AI
Self-Driving Cars
Prognosis

Practical Advances in
Artificial Intelligence and Machine Learning

Dr. Lance B. Eliot, MBA, PhD

Disclaimer: This book is presented solely for educational and entertainment purposes. The author and publisher are not offering it as legal, accounting, or other professional services advice. The author and publisher make no representations or warranties of any kind and assume no liabilities of any kind with respect to the accuracy or completeness of the contents and specifically disclaim any implied warranties of merchantability or fitness of use for a particular purpose. Neither the author nor the publisher shall be held liable or responsible to any person or entity with respect to any loss or incidental or consequential damages caused, or alleged to have been caused, directly or indirectly, by the information or programs contained herein. Every company is different and the advice and strategies contained herein may not be suitable for your situation.

DEDICATION

To my incredible son, Michael, and my incredible daughter, Lauren.

Forest fortuna adiuvat (from the Latin; good fortune favors the brave).

CONTENTS

Lance B. Eliot

ACKNOWLEDGMENTS

I have been the beneficiary of advice and counsel by many friends, colleagues, family, investors, and many others. I want to thank everyone that has aided me throughout my career. I write from the heart and the head, having experienced first-hand what it means to have others around you that support you during the good times and the tough times.

To Warren Bennis, one of my doctoral advisors and ultimately a colleague, I offer my deepest thanks and appreciation, especially for his calm and insightful wisdom and support.

To Mark Stevens and his generous efforts toward funding and supporting the USC Stevens Center for Innovation.

To Lloyd Greif and the USC Lloyd Greif Center for Entrepreneurial Studies for their ongoing encouragement of founders and entrepreneurs.

To Peter Drucker, William Wang, Aaron Levie, Peter Kim, Jon Kraft, Cindy Crawford, Jenny Ming, Steve Milligan, Chis Underwood, Frank Gehry, Buzz Aldrin, Steve Forbes, Bill Thompson, Dave Dillon, Alan Fuerstman, Larry Ellison, Jim Sinegal, John Sperling, Mark Stevenson, Anand Nallathambi, Thomas Barrack, Jr., and many other innovators and leaders that I have met and gained mightily from doing so.

Thanks to Ed Trainor, Kevin Anderson, James Hickey, Wendell Jones, Ken Harris, DuWayne Peterson, Mike Brown, Jim Thornton, Abhi Beniwal, Al Biland, John Nomura, Eliot Weinman, John Desmond, and many others for their unwavering support during my career.

And most of all thanks as always to Lauren and Michael, for their ongoing support and for having seen me writing and heard much of this material during the many months involved in writing it. To their patience and willingness to listen.

INTRODUCTION

This is a book that provides the newest innovations and the latest Artificial Intelligence (AI) advances about the emerging nature of AI-based autonomous self-driving driverless cars. Via recent advances in Artificial Intelligence (AI) and Machine Learning (ML), we are nearing the day when vehicles can control themselves and will not require and nor rely upon human intervention to perform their driving tasks (or, that <u>allow</u> for human intervention, but only *require* human intervention in very limited ways).

Similar to my other related books, which I describe in a moment and list the chapters in the Appendix A of this book, I am particularly focused on those advances that pertain to self-driving cars. The phrase "autonomous vehicles" is often used to refer to any kind of vehicle, whether it is ground-based or in the air or sea, and whether it is a cargo hauling trailer truck or a conventional passenger car. Though the aspects described in this book are certainly applicable to all kinds of autonomous vehicles, I am focused more so here on cars.

Indeed, I am especially known for my role in aiding the advancement of self-driving cars, serving currently as the Executive Director of the Cybernetic AI Self-Driving Cars Institute. In addition to writing software, designing and developing systems and software for self-driving cars, I also speak and write quite a bit about the topic. This book is a collection of some of my more advanced essays. For those of you that might have seen my essays posted elsewhere, I have updated them and integrated them into this book as one handy cohesive package.

You might be interested in companion books that I have written that provide additional key innovations and fundamentals about self-driving cars. Those books are entitled **"Introduction to Driverless Self-Driving Cars," "Advances in AI and Autonomous Vehicles: Cybernetic Self-Driving Cars," "Self-Driving Cars: "The Mother of All AI Projects," "Innovation and Thought Leadership on Self-Driving Driverless Cars," "New Advances in AI Autonomous Driverless Self-Driving Cars," "Autonomous Vehicle Driverless Self-Driving Cars and Artificial Intelligence," "Transformative Artificial Intelligence**

1

Driverless Self-Driving Cars," "Disruptive Artificial Intelligence and Driverless Self-Driving Cars, and "State-of-the-Art AI Driverless Self-Driving Cars," and "Top Trends in AI Self-Driving Cars," and "AI Innovations and Self-Driving Cars," "Crucial Advances for AI Driverless Cars," "Sociotechnical Insights and AI Driverless Cars," "Pioneering Advances for AI Driverless Cars" and "Leading Edge Trends for AI Driverless Cars," "The Cutting Edge of AI Autonomous Cars" and "The Next Wave of AI Self-Driving Cars" and "Revolutionary Innovations of AI Self-Driving Cars," and "AI Self-Driving Cars Breakthroughs," "Trailblazing Trends for AI Self-Driving Cars," "Ingenious Strides for AI Driverless Cars," "AI Self-Driving Cars Inventiveness," "Visionary Secrets of AI Driverless Cars," "Spearheading AI Self-Driving Cars," "Spurring AI Self-Driving Cars," "Avant-Garde AI Driverless Cars," "AI Self-Driving Cars Evolvement," "AI Driverless Cars Chrysalis," "Boosting AI Autonomous Cars," "AI Self-Driving Cars Trendsetting," "AI Autonomous Cars Forefront, "AI Autonomous Cars Emergence," "AI Autonomous Cars Progress," "AI Self-Driving Cars Prognosis" (they are available on Amazon). Appendix A has a listing of the chapters covered.

For this book, I am going to borrow my introduction from those companion books, since it does a good job of laying out the landscape of self-driving cars and my overall viewpoints on the topic. The remainder of this book is material that does not appear in the companion books.

INTRODUCTION TO SELF-DRIVING CARS

This is a book about self-driving cars. Someday in the future, we'll all have self-driving cars and this book will perhaps seem antiquated, but right now, we are at the forefront of the self-driving car wave. Daily news bombards us with flashes of new announcements by one car maker or another and leaves the impression that within the next few weeks or maybe months that the self-driving car will be here. A casual non-technical reader would assume from these news flashes that in fact we must be on the cusp of a true self-driving car. Here's a real news flash: We are still quite a distance from having a true self-driving car. It is years to go before we get there.

Why is that? Because a true self-driving car is akin to a moonshot. In the same manner that getting us to the moon was an incredible feat, likewise is achieving a true self-driving car. Anybody that suggests or even brashly states that the true self-driving car is nearly here should be viewed with great skepticism. Indeed, you'll see that I often tend to use the word "hogwash" or "crock" when I assess much of the decidedly *fake news* about self-driving cars.

Indeed, I've been writing a popular blog post about self-driving cars and hitting hard on those that try to wave their hands and pretend that we are on the imminent verge of true self-driving cars. For many years, I've been known as the AI Insider. Besides writing about AI, I also develop AI software. I do what I describe. It also gives me insights into what others that are doing AI are really doing versus what it is said they are doing.

Many faithful readers had asked me to pull together my insightful short essays and put them into another book, which you are now holding.

For those of you that have been reading my essays over the years, this collection not only puts them together into one handy package, I also updated the essays and added new material. For those of you that are new to the topic of self-driving cars and AI, I hope you find these essays approachable and informative. I also tend to have a writing style with a bit of a voice, and so you'll see that I am times have a wry sense of humor and poke at conformity.

As a former professor and founder of an AI research lab, I for many years wrote in the formal language of academic writing. I published in referred journals and served as an editor for several AI journals. This writing here is not of the nature, and I have adopted a different and more informal style for these essays. That being said, I also do mention from time-to-time more rigorous material on AI and encourage you all to dig into those deeper and more formal materials if so interested.

I am also an AI practitioner. This means that I write AI software for a living. Currently, I head-up the Cybernetics Self-Driving Car Institute, where we are developing AI software for self-driving cars. I am excited to also report that my son, also a software engineer, heads-up our Cybernetics Self-Driving Car Lab. What I have helped to start, and for which he is an integral part, ultimately he will carry long into the future after I have retired. My daughter, a marketing whiz, also is integral to our efforts as head of our Marketing group. She too will carry forward the legacy now being formulated.

For those of you that are reading this book and have a penchant for writing code, you might consider taking a look at the open source code available for self-driving cars. This is a handy place to start learning how to develop AI for self-driving cars. There are also many new educational courses spring forth. There is a growing body of those wanting to learn about and develop self-driving cars, and a growing body of colleges, labs, and other avenues by which you can learn about self-driving cars.

This book will provide a foundation of aspects that I think will get you ready for those kinds of more advanced training opportunities. If you've already taken those classes, you'll likely find these essays especially interesting as they offer a perspective that I am betting few other instructors or faculty offered to you. These are challenging essays that ask you to think beyond the conventional about self-driving cars.

THE MOTHER OF ALL AI PROJECTS

In June 2017, Apple CEO Tim Cook came out and finally admitted that Apple has been working on a self-driving car. As you'll see in my essays, Apple was enmeshed in secrecy about their self-driving car efforts. We have only been able to read the tea leaves and guess at what Apple has been up to. The notion of an iCar has been floating for quite a while, and self-driving engineers and researchers have been signing tight-lipped Non-Disclosure Agreements (NDA's) to work on projects at Apple that were as shrouded in mystery as any military invasion plans might be.

Tim Cook said something that many others in the Artificial Intelligence (AI) field have been saying, namely, the creation of a self-driving car has got to be the mother of all AI projects. In other words, it is in fact a tremendous moonshot for AI. If a self-driving car can be crafted and the AI works as we hope, it means that we have made incredible strides with AI and that therefore it opens many other worlds of potential breakthrough accomplishments that AI can solve.

Is this hyperbole? Am I just trying to make AI seem like a miracle worker and so provide self-aggrandizing statements for those of us writing the AI software for self-driving cars? No, it is not hyperbole. Developing a true self-driving car is really, really, really hard to do. Let me take a moment to explain why. As a side note, I realize that the Apple CEO is known for at times uttering hyperbole, and he had previously said for example that the year 2012 was "the mother of all years," and he had said that the release of iOS 10 was "the mother of all releases" – all of which does suggest he likes to use the handy "mother of" expression. But, I assure you, in terms of true self-driving cars, he has hit the nail on the head. For sure.

When you think about a moonshot and how we got to the moon, there are some identifiable characteristics and those same aspects can be applied to creating a true self-driving car. You'll notice that I keep putting the word "true" in front of the self-driving car expression. I do so because as per my essay about the various levels of self-driving cars, there are some self-driving cars that are only somewhat of a self-driving car. The somewhat versions are ones that require a human driver to be ready to intervene. In my view, that's not a true self-driving car. A true self-driving car is one that requires no human driver intervention at all. It is a car that can entirely undertake via automation the driving task without any human driver needed. This is the essence of what is known as a Level 5 self-driving car. We are currently at the Level 2 and Level 3 mark, and not yet at Level 5.

Getting to the moon involved aspects such as having big stretch goals, incremental progress, experimentation, innovation, and so on. Let's review how this applied to the moonshot of the bygone era, and how it applies to the self-driving car moonshot of today.

Big Stretch Goal

Trying to take a human and deliver the human to the moon, and bring them back, safely, was an extremely large stretch goal at the time. No one knew whether it could be done. The technology wasn't available yet. The cost was huge. The determination would need to be fierce. Etc. To reach a Level 5 self-driving car is going to be the same. It is a big stretch goal. We can readily get to the Level 3, and we are able to see the Level 4 just up ahead, but a Level 5 is still an unknown as to if it is doable. It should eventually be doable and in the same way that we thought we'd eventually get to the moon, but when it will occur is a different story.

Incremental Progress

Getting to the moon did not happen overnight in one fell swoop. It took years and years of incremental progress to get there. Likewise for self-driving cars. Google has famously been striving to get to the Level 5, and pretty much been willing to forgo dealing with the intervening levels, but most of the other self-driving car makers are doing the incremental route. Let's get a good Level 2 and a somewhat Level 3 going. Then, let's improve the Level 3 and get a somewhat Level 4 going. Then, let's improve the Level 4 and finally arrive at a Level 5. This seems to be the prevalent way that we are going to achieve the true self-driving car.

Experimentation

You likely know that there were various experiments involved in perfecting the approach and technology to get to the moon. As per making incremental progress, we first tried to see if we could get a rocket to go into space and safety return, then put a monkey in there, then with a human, then we went all the way to the moon but didn't land, and finally we arrived at the mission that actually landed on the moon. Self-driving cars are the same way. We are doing simulations of self-driving cars. We do testing of self-driving cars on private land under controlled situations. We do testing of self-driving cars on public roadways, often having to meet regulatory requirements including for example having an engineer or equivalent in the car to take over the controls if needed. And so on. Experiments big and small are needed to figure out what works and what doesn't.

Innovation

There are already some advances in AI that are allowing us to progress toward self-driving cars. We are going to need even more advances. Innovation in all aspects of technology are going to be required to achieve a true self-driving car. By no means do we already have everything in-hand that we need to get there. Expect new inventions and new approaches, new algorithms, etc.

Setbacks

Most of the pundits are avoiding talking about potential setbacks in the progress toward self-driving cars. Getting to the moon involved many setbacks, some of which you never have heard of and were buried at the time so as to not dampen enthusiasm and funding for getting to the moon. A recurring theme in many of my included essays is that there are going to be setbacks as we try to arrive at a true self-driving car. Take a deep breath and be ready. I just hope the setbacks don't completely stop progress. I am sure that it will cause progress to alter in a manner that we've not yet seen in the self-driving car field. I liken the self-driving car of today to the excitement everyone had for Uber when it first got going. Today, we have a different view of Uber and with each passing day there are more regulations to the ride sharing business and more concerns raised. The darling child only stays a darling until finally that child acts up. It will happen the same with self-driving cars.

SELF-DRIVING CARS CHALLENGES

But what exactly makes things so hard to have a true self-driving car, you might be asking. You have seen cruise control for years and years. You've lately seen cars that can do parallel parking. You've seen YouTube videos of Tesla drivers that put their hands out the window as their car zooms along the highway, and seen to therefore be in a self-driving car. Aren't we just needing to put a few more sensors onto a car and then we'll have in-hand a true self-driving car? Nope.

Consider for a moment the nature of the driving task. We don't just let anyone at any age drive a car. Worldwide, most countries won't license a driver until the age of 18, though many do allow a learner's permit at the age of 15 or 16. Some suggest that a younger age would be physically too small to reach the controls of the car. Though this might be the case, we could easily adjust the controls to allow for younger aged and thus smaller stature. It's not their physical size that matters. It's their cognitive development that matters.

To drive a car, you need to be able to reason about the car, what the car can and cannot do. You need to know how to operate the car. You need to know about how other cars on the road drive. You need to know what is allowed in driving such as speed limits and driving within marked lanes. You need to be able to react to situations and be able to avoid getting into accidents. You need to ascertain when to hit your brakes, when to steer clear of a pedestrian, and how to keep from ramming that motorcyclist that just cut you off.

Many of us had taken courses on driving. We studied about driving and took driver training. We had to take a test and pass it to be able to drive. The point being that though most adults take the driving task for granted, and we often "mindlessly" drive our cars, there is a significant amount of cognitive effort that goes into driving a car. After a while, it becomes second nature. You don't especially think about how you drive, you just do it. But, if you watch a novice driver, say a teenager learning to drive, you suddenly realize that there is a lot more complexity to it than we seem to realize.

Furthermore, driving is a very serious task. I recall when my daughter and son first learned to drive. They are both very conscientious people. They wanted to make sure that whatever they did, they did well, and that they did not harm anyone. Every day, when you get into a car, it is probably around 4,000 pounds of hefty metal and plastics (about two tons), and it is a lethal weapon. Think about it. You drive down the street in an object that weighs two tons and with the engine it can accelerate and ram into anything you want to hit. The damage a car can inflict is very scary. Both my children were surprised that they were being given the right to maneuver this monster of a beast that could cause tremendous harm entirely by merely letting go of the steering wheel for a moment or taking your eyes off the road.

In fact, in the United States alone there are about 30,000 deaths per year by auto accidents, which is around 100 per day. Given that there are about 263 million cars in the United States, I am actually more amazed that the number of fatalities is not a lot higher. During my morning commute, I look at all the thousands of cars on the freeway around me, and I think that if all of them decided to go zombie and drive in a crazy maniac way, there would be many people dead. Somehow, incredibly, each day, most people drive relatively safely. To me, that's a miracle right there. Getting millions and millions of people to be safe and sane when behind the wheel of a two ton mobile object, it's a feat that we as a society should admire with pride.

So, hopefully you are in agreement that the driving task requires a great deal of cognition. You don't' need to be especially smart to drive a car, and we've done quite a bit to make car driving viable for even the average dolt. There isn't an IQ test that you need to take to drive a car. If you can read and write, and pass a test, you pretty much can legally drive a car. There are of course some that drive a car and are not legally permitted to do so, plus there are private areas such as farms where drivers are young, but for public roadways in the United States, you can be generally of average intelligence (or less) and be able to legally drive.

This though makes it seem like the cognitive effort must not be much. If the cognitive effort was truly hard, wouldn't we only have Einstein's that could drive a car? We have made sure to keep the driving task as simple as we can, by making the controls easy and relatively standardized, and by having roads that are relatively standardized, and so on. It is as though Disneyland has put their Autopia into the real-world, by us all as a society agreeing that roads will be a certain way, and we'll all abide by the various rules of driving.

A modest cognitive task by a human is still something that stymies AI. You certainly know that AI has been able to beat chess players and be good at other kinds of games. This type of narrow cognition is not what car driving is about. Car driving is much wider. It requires knowledge about the world, which a chess playing AI system does not need to know. The cognitive aspects of driving are on the one hand seemingly simple, but at the same time require layer upon layer of knowledge about cars, people, roads, rules, and a myriad of other "common sense" aspects. We don't have any AI systems today that have that same kind of breadth and depth of awareness and knowledge.

As revealed in my essays, the self-driving car of today is using trickery to do particular tasks. It is all very narrow in operation. Plus, it currently assumes that a human driver is ready to intervene. It is like a child that we have taught to stack blocks, but we are needed to be right there in case the child stacks them too high and they begin to fall over. AI of today is brittle, it is narrow, and it does not approach the cognitive abilities of humans. This is why the true self-driving car is somewhere out in the future.

Another aspect to the driving task is that it is not solely a mind exercise. You do need to use your senses to drive. You use your eyes a vision sensors to see the road ahead. You vision capability is like a streaming video, which your brain needs to continually analyze as you drive. Where is the road? Is there a pedestrian in the way? Is there another car ahead of you? Your senses are relying a flood of info to your brain. Self-driving cars are trying to do the same, by using cameras, radar, ultrasound, and lasers. This is an attempt at mimicking how humans have senses and sensory apparatus.

Thus, the driving task is mental and physical. You use your senses, you use your arms and legs to manipulate the controls of the car, and you use your brain to assess the sensory info and direct your limbs to act upon the controls of the car. This all happens instantly. If you've ever perhaps gotten something in your eye and only had one eye available to drive with, you suddenly realize how dependent upon vision you are. If you have a broken foot with a cast, you suddenly realize how hard it is to control the brake pedal and the accelerator. If you've taken medication and your brain is maybe sluggish, you suddenly realize how much mental strain is required to drive a car.

An AI system that plays chess only needs to be focused on playing chess. The physical aspects aren't important because usually a human moves the chess pieces or the chessboard is shown on an electronic display. Using AI for a more life-and-death task such as analyzing MRI images of patients, this again does not require physical capabilities and instead is done by examining images of bits.

Driving a car is a true life-and-death task. It is a use of AI that can easily and at any moment produce death. For those colleagues of mine that are developing this AI, as am I, we need to keep in mind the somber aspects of this. We are producing software that will have in its virtual hands the lives of the occupants of the car, and the lives of those in other nearby cars, and the lives of nearby pedestrians, etc. Chess is not usually a life-or-death matter.

Driving is all around us. Cars are everywhere. Most of today's AI applications involve only a small number of people. Or, they are behind the scenes and we as humans have other recourse if the AI messes up. AI that is driving a car at 80 miles per hour on a highway had better not mess up. The consequences are grave. Multiply this by the number of cars, if we could put magically self-driving into every car in the USA, we'd have AI running in the 263 million cars. That's a lot of AI spread around. This is AI on a massive scale that we are not doing today and that offers both promise and potential peril.

There are some that want AI for self-driving cars because they envision a world without any car accidents. They envision a world in which there is no car congestion and all cars cooperate with each other. These are wonderful utopian visions.

They are also very misleading. The adoption of self-driving cars is going to be incremental and not overnight. We cannot economically just junk all existing cars. Nor are we going to be able to affordably retrofit existing cars. It is more likely that self-driving cars will be built into new cars and that over many years of gradual replacement of existing cars that we'll see the mix of self-driving cars become substantial in the real-world.

In these essays, I have tried to offer technological insights without being overly technical in my description, and also blended the business, societal, and economic aspects too. Technologists need to consider the non-technological impacts of what they do. Non-technologists should be aware of what is being developed.

We all need to work together to collectively be prepared for the enormous disruption and transformative aspects of true self-driving cars. We all need to be involved in this mother of all AI projects.

WHAT THIS BOOK PROVIDES

What does this book provide to you? It introduces many of the key elements about self-driving cars and does so with an AI based perspective. I weave together technical and non-technical aspects, readily going from being concerned about the cognitive capabilities of the driving task and how the technology is embodying this into self-driving cars, and in the next breath I discuss the societal and economic aspects.

They are all intertwined because that's the way reality is. You cannot separate out the technology per se, and instead must consider it within the milieu of what is being invented and innovated, and do so with a mindset towards the contemporary mores and culture that shape what we are doing and what we hope to do.

WHY THIS BOOK

I wrote this book to try and bring to the public view many aspects about self-driving cars that nobody seems to be discussing.

For business leaders that are either involved in making self-driving cars or that are going to leverage self-driving cars, I hope that this book will enlighten you as to the risks involved and ways in which you should be strategizing about how to deal with those risks.

For entrepreneurs, startups and other businesses that want to enter into the self-driving car market that is emerging, I hope this book sparks your interest in doing so, and provides some sense of what might be prudent to pursue.

For researchers that study self-driving cars, I hope this book spurs your interest in the risks and safety issues of self-driving cars, and also nudges you toward conducting research on those aspects.

For students in computer science or related disciplines, I hope this book will provide you with interesting and new ideas and material, for which you might conduct research or provide some career direction insights for you.

For AI companies and high-tech companies pursuing self-driving cars, this book will hopefully broaden your view beyond just the mere coding and development needed to make self-driving cars.

For all readers, I hope that you will find the material in this book to be stimulating. Some of it will be repetitive of things you already know. But I am pretty sure that you'll also find various eureka moments whereby you'll discover a new technique or approach that you had not earlier thought of. I am also betting that there will be material that forces you to rethink some of your current practices.

I am not saying you will suddenly have an epiphany and change what you are doing. I do think though that you will reconsider or perhaps revisit what you are doing.

For anyone choosing to use this book for teaching purposes, please take a look at my suggestions for doing so, as described in the Appendix. I have found the material handy in courses that I have taught, and likewise other faculty have told me that they have found the material handy, in some cases as extended readings and in other instances as a core part of their course (depending on the nature of the class).

In my writing for this book, I have tried carefully to blend both the practitioner and the academic styles of writing. It is not as dense as is typical academic journal writing, but at the same time offers depth by going into the nuances and trade-offs of various practices.

The word "deep" is in vogue today, meaning getting deeply into a subject or topic, and so is the word "unpack" which means to tease out the underlying aspects of a subject or topic. I have sought to offer material that addresses an issue or topic by going relatively deeply into it and make sure that it is well unpacked.

In any book about AI, it is difficult to use our everyday words without having some of them be misinterpreted. Specifically, it is easy to anthropomorphize AI. When I say that an AI system "knows" something, I do not want you to construe that the AI system has sentience and "knows" in the same way that humans do. They aren't that way, as yet. I have tried to use quotes around such words from time-to-time to emphasize that the words I am using should not be misinterpreted to ascribe true human intelligence to the AI systems that we know of today. If I used quotes around all such words, the book would be very difficult to read, and so I am doing so judiciously. Please keep that in mind as you read the material, thanks.

Some of the material is time-based in terms of covering underway activities, and though some of it might decay, nonetheless I believe you'll find the material useful and informative.

COMPANION BOOKS

1. **"Introduction to Driverless Self-Driving Cars"** by Dr. Lance Eliot
2. **"Innovation and Thought Leadership on Self-Driving Driverless Cars"** by Dr. Lance Eliot
3. **"Advances in AI and Autonomous Vehicles: Cybernetic Self-Driving Cars"** by Dr. Lance Eliot
4. **"Self-Driving Cars: The Mother of All AI Projects"** by Dr. Lance Eliot
5. **"New Advances in AI Autonomous Driverless Self-Driving Cars"** by Dr. Lance Eliot
6. **"Autonomous Vehicle Driverless Self-Driving Cars and Artificial Intelligence"** by Dr. Lance Eliot and Michael B. Eliot
7. **"Transformative Artificial Intelligence Driverless Self-Driving Cars"** by Dr. Lance Eliot
8. **"Disruptive Artificial Intelligence and Driverless Self-Driving Cars"** by Dr. Lance Eliot
9. "State-of-the-Art AI Driverless Self-Driving Cars" by Dr. Lance Eliot
10. "**Top Trends in AI Self-Driving Cars**" by Dr. Lance Eliot
11. **"AI Innovations and Self-Driving Cars"** by Dr. Lance Eliot
12. **"Crucial Advances for AI Driverless Cars"** by Dr. Lance Eliot
13. **"Sociotechnical Insights and AI Driverless Cars"** by Dr. Lance Eliot.
14. **"Pioneering Advances for AI Driverless Cars"** by Dr. Lance Eliot
15. **"Leading Edge Trends for AI Driverless Cars"** by Dr. Lance Eliot
16. **"The Cutting Edge of AI Autonomous Cars"** by Dr. Lance Eliot
17. **"The Next Wave of AI Self-Driving Cars"** by Dr. Lance Eliot
18. **"Revolutionary Innovations of AI Driverless Cars"** by Dr. Lance Eliot
19. **"AI Self-Driving Cars Breakthroughs"** by Dr. Lance Eliot
20. **"Trailblazing Trends for AI Self-Driving Cars"** by Dr. Lance Eliot
21. **"Ingenious Strides for AI Driverless Cars"** by Dr. Lance Eliot
22. **"AI Self-Driving Cars Inventiveness"** by Dr. Lance Eliot
23. **"Visionary Secrets of AI Driverless Cars"** by Dr. Lance Eliot
24. **"Spearheading AI Self-Driving Cars"** by Dr. Lance Eliot
25. **"Spurring AI Self-Driving Cars"** by Dr. Lance Eliot
26. **"Avant-Garde AI Driverless Cars"** by Dr. Lance Eliot
27. **"AI Self-Driving Cars Evolvement"** by Dr. Lance Eliot
28. **"AI Driverless Cars Chrysalis"** by Dr. Lance Eliot
29. **"Boosting AI Autonomous Cars"** by Dr. Lance Eliot
30. **"AI Self-Driving Cars Trendsetting"** by Dr. Lance Eliot
31. **"AI Autonomous Cars Forefront"** by Dr. Lance Eliot
32. **"AI Autonomous Cars Emergence"** by Dr. Lance Eliot
33. **"AI Autonomous Cars Progress"** by Dr. Lance Eliot
34. **"AI Self-Driving Cars Prognosis"** by Dr. Lance Eliot

These books are available on Amazon and at other major global booksellers.

CHAPTER 1

ELIOT FRAMEWORK FOR AI SELF-DRIVING CARS

CHAPTER 1

ELIOT FRAMEWORK FOR AI SELF-DRIVING CARS

This chapter is a core foundational aspect for understanding AI self-driving cars and I have used this same chapter in several of my other books to introduce the reader to essential elements of this field. Once you've read this chapter, you'll be prepared to read the rest of the material since the foundational essence of the components of autonomous AI driverless self-driving cars will have been established for you.

—————

When I give presentations about self-driving cars and teach classes on the topic, I have found it helpful to provide a framework around which the various key elements of self-driving cars can be understood and organized (see diagram at the end of this chapter). The framework needs to be simple enough to convey the overarching elements, but at the same time not so simple that it belies the true complexity of self-driving cars. As such, I am going to describe the framework here and try to offer in a thousand words (or more!) what the framework diagram itself intends to portray.

The core elements on the diagram are numbered for ease of reference. The numbering does not suggest any kind of prioritization of the elements. Each element is crucial. Each element has a purpose, and otherwise would not be included in the framework. For some self-driving cars, a particular element might be more important or somehow distinguished in comparison to other self-driving cars.

You could even use the framework to rate a particular self-driving car, doing so by gauging how well it performs in each of the elements of the framework. I will describe each of the elements, one at a time. After doing so, I'll discuss aspects that illustrate how the elements interact and perform during the overall effort of a self-driving car.

At the Cybernetic Self-Driving Car Institute, we use the framework to keep track of what we are working on, and how we are developing software that fills in what is needed to achieve Level 5 self-driving cars.

D-01: Sensor Capture

Let's start with the one element that often gets the most attention in the press about self-driving cars, namely, the sensory devices for a self-driving car.

On the framework, the box labeled as D-01 indicates "Sensor Capture" and refers to the processes of the self-driving car that involve collecting data from the myriad of sensors that are used for a self-driving car. The types of devices typically involved are listed, such as the use of mono cameras, stereo cameras, LIDAR devices, radar systems, ultrasonic devices, GPS, IMU, and so on.

These devices are tasked with obtaining data about the status of the self-driving car and the world around it. Some of the devices are continually providing updates, while others of the devices await an indication by the self-driving car that the device is supposed to collect data. The data might be first transformed in some fashion by the device itself, or it might instead be fed directly into the sensor capture as raw data. At that point, it might be up to the sensor capture processes to do transformations on the data. This all varies depending upon the nature of the devices being used and how the devices were designed and developed.

D-02: Sensor Fusion

Imagine that your eyeballs receive visual images, your nose receives odors, your ears receive sounds, and in essence each of your distinct sensory devices is getting some form of input. The input befits the nature of the device. Likewise, for a self-driving car, the cameras provide visual images, the radar returns radar reflections, and so on.

Each device provides the data as befits what the device does.

At some point, using the analogy to humans, you need to merge together what your eyes see, what your nose smells, what your ears hear, and piece it all together into a larger sense of what the world is all about and what is happening around you. Sensor fusion is the action of taking the singular aspects from each of the devices and putting them together into a larger puzzle.

Sensor fusion is a tough task. There are some devices that might not be working at the time of the sensor capture. Or, there might some devices that are unable to report well what they have detected. Again, using a human analogy, suppose you are in a dark room and so your eyes cannot see much. At that point, you might need to rely more so on your ears and what you hear. The same is true for a self-driving car. If the cameras are obscured due to snow and sleet, it might be that the radar can provide a greater indication of what the external conditions consist of.

In the case of a self-driving car, there can be a plethora of such sensory devices. Each is reporting what it can. Each might have its difficulties. Each might have its limitations, such as how far ahead it can detect an object. All of these limitations need to be considered during the sensor fusion task.

D-03: Virtual World Model

For humans, we presumably keep in our minds a model of the world around us when we are driving a car. In your mind, you know that the car is going at say 60 miles per hour and that you are on a freeway. You have a model in your mind that your car is surrounded by other cars, and that there are lanes to the freeway. Your model is not only based on what you can see, hear, etc., but also what you know about the nature of the world. You know that at any moment that car ahead of you can smash on its brakes, or the car behind you can ram into your car, or that the truck in the next lane might swerve into your lane.

The AI of the self-driving car needs to have a virtual world model, which it then keeps updated with whatever it is receiving from the sensor fusion, which received its input from the sensor capture and the sensory devices.

D-04: System Action Plan

By having a virtual world model, the AI of the self-driving car is able to keep track of where the car is and what is happening around the car. In addition, the AI needs to determine what to do next. Should the self-driving car hit its brakes? Should the self-driving car stay in its lane or swerve into the lane to the left? Should the self-driving car accelerate or slow down?

A system action plan needs to be prepared by the AI of the self-driving car. The action plan specifies what actions should be taken. The actions need to pertain to the status of the virtual world model. Plus, the actions need to be realizable.

This realizability means that the AI cannot just assert that the self-driving car should suddenly sprout wings and fly. Instead, the AI must be bound by whatever the self-driving car can actually do, such as coming to a halt in a distance of X feet at a speed of Y miles per hour, rather than perhaps asserting that the self-driving car come to a halt in 0 feet as though it could instantaneously come to a stop while it is in motion.

D-05: Controls Activation

The system action plan is implemented by activating the controls of the car to act according to what the plan stipulates. This might mean that the accelerator control is commanded to increase the speed of the car. Or, the steering control is commanded to turn the steering wheel 30 degrees to the left or right.

One question arises as to whether or not the controls respond as they are commanded to do. In other words, suppose the AI has commanded the accelerator to increase, but for some reason it does not do so. Or, maybe it tries to do so, but the speed of the car does not increase. The controls activation feeds back into the virtual world model, and simultaneously the virtual world model is getting updated from the sensors, the sensor capture, and the sensor fusion. This allows the AI to ascertain what has taken place as a result of the controls being commanded to take some kind of action.

By the way, please keep in mind that though the diagram seems to have a linear progression to it, the reality is that these are all aspects of the self-driving car that are happening in parallel and simultaneously. The sensors are capturing data, meanwhile the sensor fusion is taking place, meanwhile the virtual model is being updated, meanwhile the system action plan is being formulated and reformulated, meanwhile the controls are being activated.

This is the same as a human being that is driving a car. They are eyeballing the road, meanwhile they are fusing in their mind the sights, sounds, etc., meanwhile their mind is updating their model of the world around them, meanwhile they are formulating an action plan of what to do, and meanwhile they are pushing their foot onto the pedals and steering the car. In the normal course of driving a car, you are doing all of these at once. I mention this so that when you look at the diagram, you will think of the boxes as processes that are all happening at the same time, and not as though only one happens and then the next.

They are shown diagrammatically in a simplistic manner to help comprehend what is taking place. You though should also realize that they are working in parallel and simultaneous with each other. This is a tough aspect in that the inter-element communications involve latency and other aspects that must be taken into account. There can be delays in one element updating and then sharing its latest status with other elements.

D-06: Automobile & CAN

Contemporary cars use various automotive electronics and a Controller Area Network (CAN) to serve as the components that underlie the driving aspects of a car. There are Electronic Control Units (ECU's) which control subsystems of the car, such as the engine, the brakes, the doors, the windows, and so on.

The elements D-01, D-02, D-03, D-04, D-05 are layered on top of the D-06, and must be aware of the nature of what the D-06 is able to do and not do.

D-07: In-Car Commands

Humans are going to be occupants in self-driving cars. In a Level 5 self-driving car, there must be some form of communication that takes place between the humans and the self-driving car. For example, I go into a self-driving car and tell it that I want to be driven over to Disneyland, and along the way I want to stop at In-and-Out Burger. The self-driving car now parses what I've said and tries to then establish a means to carry out my wishes.

In-car commands can happen at any time during a driving journey. Though my example was about an in-car command when I first got into my self-driving car, it could be that while the self-driving car is carrying out the journey that I change my mind. Perhaps after getting stuck in traffic, I tell the self-driving car to forget about getting the burgers and just head straight over to the theme park. The self-driving car needs to be alert to in-car commands throughout the journey.

D-08: V2X Communications

We will ultimately have self-driving cars communicating with each other, doing so via V2V (Vehicle-to-Vehicle) communications. We will also have self-driving cars that communicate with the roadways and other aspects of the transportation infrastructure, doing so via V2I (Vehicle-to-Infrastructure).

The variety of ways in which a self-driving car will be communicating with other cars and infrastructure is being called V2X, whereby the letter X means whatever else we identify as something that a car should or would want to communicate with. The V2X communications will be taking place simultaneous with everything else on the diagram, and those other elements will need to incorporate whatever it gleans from those V2X communications.

D-09: Deep Learning

The use of Deep Learning permeates all other aspects of the self-driving car. The AI of the self-driving car will be using deep learning to do a better job at the systems action plan, and at the controls activation, and at the sensor fusion, and so on.

Currently, the use of artificial neural networks is the most prevalent form of deep learning. Based on large swaths of data, the neural networks attempt to "learn" from the data and therefore direct the efforts of the self-driving car accordingly.

D-10: Tactical AI

Tactical AI is the element of dealing with the moment-to-moment driving of the self-driving car. Is the self-driving car staying in its lane of the freeway? Is the car responding appropriately to the controls commands? Are the sensory devices working?

For human drivers, the tactical equivalent can be seen when you watch a novice driver such as a teenager that is first driving. They are focused on the mechanics of the driving task, keeping their eye on the road while also trying to properly control the car.

D-11: Strategic AI

The Strategic AI aspects of a self-driving car are dealing with the larger picture of what the self-driving car is trying to do. If I had asked that the self-driving car take me to Disneyland, there is an overall journey map that needs to be kept and maintained.

There is an interaction between the Strategic AI and the Tactical AI. The Strategic AI is wanting to keep on the mission of the driving, while the Tactical AI is focused on the particulars underway in the driving effort. If the Tactical AI seems to wander away from the overarching mission, the Strategic AI wants to see why and get things back on track. If the Tactical AI realizes that there is something amiss on the self-driving car, it needs to alert the Strategic AI accordingly and have an adjustment to the overarching mission that is underway.

D-12: Self-Aware AI

Very few of the self-driving cars being developed are including a Self-Aware AI element, which we at the Cybernetic Self-Driving Car Institute believe is crucial to Level 5 self-driving cars.

The Self-Aware AI element is intended to watch over itself, in the sense that the AI is making sure that the AI is working as intended. Suppose you had a human driving a car, and they were starting to drive erratically. Hopefully, their own self-awareness would make them realize they themselves are driving poorly, such as perhaps starting to fall asleep after having been driving for hours on end. If you had a passenger in the car, they might be able to alert the driver if the driver is starting to do something amiss. This is exactly what the Self-Aware

AI element tries to do, it becomes the overseer of the AI, and tries to detect when the AI has become faulty or confused, and then find ways to overcome the issue.

D-13: Economic

The economic aspects of a self-driving car are not per se a technology aspect of a self-driving car, but the economics do indeed impact the nature of a self-driving car. For example, the cost of outfitting a self-driving car with every kind of possible sensory device is prohibitive, and so choices need to be made about which devices are used. And, for those sensory devices chosen, whether they would have a full set of features or a more limited set of features.

We are going to have self-driving cars that are at the low-end of a consumer cost point, and others at the high-end of a consumer cost point. You cannot expect that the self-driving car at the low-end is going to be as robust as the one at the high-end. I realize that many of the self-driving car pundits are acting as though all self-driving cars will be the same, but they won't be. Just like anything else, we are going to have self-driving cars that have a range of capabilities. Some will be better than others. Some will be safer than others. This is the way of the real-world, and so we need to be thinking about the economics aspects when considering the nature of self-driving cars.

D-14: Societal

This component encompasses the societal aspects of AI which also impacts the technology of self-driving cars. For example, the famous Trolley Problem involves what choices should a self-driving car make when faced with life-and-death matters. If the self-driving car is about to either hit a child standing in the roadway, or instead ram into a tree at the side of the road and possibly kill the humans in the self-driving car, which choice should be made?

We need to keep in mind the societal aspects will underlie the AI of the self-driving car. Whether we are aware of it explicitly or not, the AI will have embedded into it various societal assumptions.

D-15: Innovation

I included the notion of innovation into the framework because we can anticipate that whatever a self-driving car consists of, it will continue to be innovated over time. The self-driving cars coming out in the next several years will undoubtedly be different and less innovative than the versions that come out in ten years hence, and so on.

Framework Overall

For those of you that want to learn about self-driving cars, you can potentially pick a particular element and become specialized in that aspect. Some engineers are focusing on the sensory devices. Some engineers focus on the controls activation. And so on. There are specialties in each of the elements.

Researchers are likewise specializing in various aspects. For example, there are researchers that are using Deep Learning to see how best it can be used for sensor fusion. There are other researchers that are using Deep Learning to derive good System Action Plans. Some are studying how to develop AI for the Strategic aspects of the driving task, while others are focused on the Tactical aspects.

A well-prepared all-around software developer that is involved in self-driving cars should be familiar with all of the elements, at least to the degree that they know what each element does. This is important since whatever piece of the pie that the software developer works on, they need to be knowledgeable about what the other elements are doing.

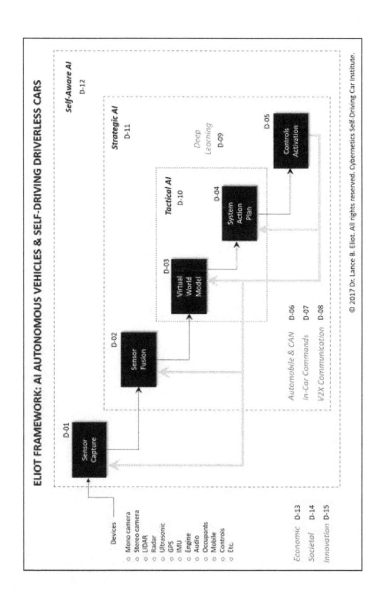

CHAPTER 2
ROADKILL
AND
AI SELF-DRIVING CARS

CHAPTER 2

ROADKILL
AND AI SELF-DRIVING CARS

For self-driving driverless autonomous cars, the more they are able to contend with a myriad of driving situations the better off we all will be.

Right now, most of the automakers and tech firms developing autonomous cars are primarily dealing with the straightforward and everyday elements of driving a car. This includes staying in your car lane, making turns that don't hit anything, and otherwise performing the rudiments of driving that say a novice teenager learning to drive might do.

What makes a novice teenager quite a bit different from today's AI driving systems is that the teenager has common sense reasoning, which I realize you might want to argue as to the extent, but putting aside such off-hand smarmy remarks, I think we can all agree that a teenager is a thinking capacity human being and will try to figure out what to do when encountering novel driving situations. Thus, even though they might have been taught just the core basics of the driving task, they are relatively adept at adjusting and coping with beyond-the-norm encounters.

The Famous Pogo Stick Edge Case

Imagine driving down a street and all of a sudden there is a person on a pogo stick, bouncing up and down and doing so in the bicycle lane of the road. In case you are questioning the possibility of such a happening, you might find of idle interest that some believe that the next big mobility fad after the advent of motorized scooters will be motorized pogo sticks. Admittedly, this seems somewhat farfetched as a populous gaining trend, and we'll have to see if there is really widespread attraction to such a springy mode of transport.

In any case, for a human being driving a car, including a novice teenager, we would likely instantly recognize that this was a human being on a pogo stick and they are of some potential danger to themselves and to the car because the person is pogoing in the street.

At any moment, the pogoing person might veer further into the path of the cars. Or, maybe the pogoing person will fall down and in so doing fall in front of the cars. Or, another car driver might get spooked by the pogoing actions and make some erratic maneuver with their car. Generally, an astute human driver would go on alert, keeping their eyes on the possibly errant pogoing person, meanwhile surveying the driving scene to detect what to do if the pogo person goes amuck, including whether as a driver it might be possible or prudent to maneuver into another lane away from the interloper.

All of those driving related actions are not easily embodied into an AI system. You and I take for granted the scenario that I've described and shrug our shoulders that it's just another day of driving on the wild and at times unpredictable traffic that we come across.

Not so for the AI system. Without any kind of common-sense reasoning, anytime an unusual situation brews, the AI is often thrown for a loop as to what is occurring. In the autonomous car industry, these novel or unusual situations are considered edge cases or corner cases. This means that driving actions beyond the core or basics are something that sits at the edge or corner of what the AI needs to be able to handle.

There is no definitive standard or accepted listing that states what constitutes an edge or corner case. It's up the eye of the beholder in terms of AI developers that might claim that a particular driving scenario is an edge case or not so.

Qualms About Relying On Public Roadway Tryouts

One of the criticisms of today's roadway tryouts of self-driving cars is that they by-and-large aren't prepared as yet to handle edge cases.

If the only means used to learn about edge cases and how to cope with them is due to trial-and-error, it suggests that a self-driving car might need to go millions upon millions of miles, perhaps billions upon billions, maybe even trillions, before it would have covered some overall proportion of edge or corner cases.

To give you a sense of the distances traveled with autonomous cars on public roadways, Waymo's self-driving car efforts, which are considered the furthest along in driverless cars, have amassed somewhere around 10 million miles. For human drivers, we collectively drive about 3.2 trillion miles annually in the United States alone. As might be evident, the VMT (vehicle miles traveled) for autonomous cars to-date is puny, though some would be quick to point out that there are simulations also being done of driverless cars and therefore hundreds of millions of "virtual" miles are being racked-up (if you agree that simulations are valid and essentially equivalent to actual roadway miles).

When simulating the act of driving, you need to come up with the potential edge cases or corner cases that you might imagine will someday be encountered on the roadway. As such, there are those that suggest that the simulations aren't necessarily able to portray a sufficiently complete set of those novel or unusual driving situations (since it requires some human that can dream them up, or research to find out what oddities have happened on the highways and byways).

It's the classic you don't know what you don't know kind of claimed limitation.

Let's consider a fascinating edge case, the roadkill matter, and an added twist involving roadkill cuisine.

California Proposing To Regulate Roadkill Cuisine

Here in California, there is a bill proposed that would enact a new law around the roadkill that occurs when drivers ram into animals that have darted onto the roadway.

A somewhat staggering number is that in California each year there are an estimated 20,000 deer killed by roadway incidents. I realize you might be puzzled and wondering whether deer are stalking the streets of downtown Los Angeles, but you need to keep in mind that California is a large state and has pockets of dense city populations that are really just a fraction of the total geography of the state (our mountains, wooded areas, and agricultural areas are the bulk of the landscape).

In a bit of tongue and cheek, the bill is being labeled as meals-under-wheels (get it, not the conventional meals-on-wheels, instead meals-under-wheels, what jokesters!).

Here's the notion. If you ram into an animal such as a deer, you will be able to legally grab-up the deceased beast and take it home for your Sunday dinner or maybe dine on it for lunch at work the next day. For allowing you to legally do so, you also need to use a state-provided mobile app to officially report what you hit, where you struck the animal, and include other registration related info.

I suppose this sounds like another strange idea emanating from California.

The logic though is that by getting the human drivers to report on the animal crushing matter, the state will be able to better understand the true extent of where the roadkills are taking place, allowing the state to do better planning for the future prevention of such matters or otherwise get their hands around the magnitude and locations of greatest concern. Presumably, people are unlikely to voluntarily report these incidents unless they have a means to do so (the mobile app) and have a bona fide incentive to do so (you get to keep and eat the roadkill).

Believe it or not, PETA and various environmentalists seem to be on-board with the proposed regulation. Generally, the feeling is that this will help via the environmental tracking and prompt proactive actions taken to reduce the chances of animals becoming roadkill, plus an animal that is struck and then dead anyway might as well be turned into useful meat to feed others. A kind of win-win, if you are willing to see it that way.

Highway harvesting like this is not unique to California, and states such as Idaho, Oregon, Montana, and others provide variant laws similar to this.

Not everyone supports these kinds of regulations, including worries that it might prompt human drivers to purposely runover animals that otherwise could have safely been avoided, plus the traffic hazard of stopping your car to go pick-up the carcass, plus the potential for illnesses that might arise from later eating these deceased animals, etc.

Edge Case Of The Roadkill Cuisine

Recast the highway harvesting or roadway cuisine in light of the advent of autonomous cars.

When you hear about these kinds of novel or unusual driving circumstances, the question that you should right away ask is: "What would a self-driving driverless autonomous car do?"

Or, if you prefer, the shorter version is: "What would the AI do?"

At this time, few of the autonomous car AI systems are prepared to deal well with hitting an animal.

Some of the software would not detect that it had hit an animal, while other software would detect the animal up ahead (possibly), realize it was going to be struck, and the action of the car as to what the AI will do could vary quite a bit.

The AI might try to radically swerve to avoid the animal, or hit the brakes, though whether the AI has also calculated the chances of having a car behind it ram into the rear of the self-driving car or whether a car in an adjacent lane driven by a human will deal with a swerving driverless car, well, some AI systems are programmed for this and some are not as yet.

AI developers that are using Machine Learning or Deep Learning for having the AI be somewhat self-taught are expecting that the more miles driven by a driverless car the more that it will encounter this kind of situation and then "learn" how to deal with it. There is though rightful skepticism whether the AI can really gauge what needs to be done, simply by pattern matching of prior similar incidents, due to the variability of how things playout. One might argue that a programmatic approach, devised by human AI developers, provides a more robust and quicker way to prepare the AI for these edge cases.

Consider too that with the proposed regulation, the passenger in the driverless car might want to have the AI stop the car after having hit the animal, back-up or turnaround and go back to the carcass, and allow the human to get out of the self-driving car and somehow affix or place the deceased animal into or onto the vehicle. Presumably, the human would then want to invoke the state mobile app to report the incident and have the self-driving car proceed on its journey.

The AI would need to be adept enough that via its Natural Language Processing capability, akin to an Alexa or Siri kind of verbal interaction, it would be able to have the human passenger orally utter a request about how the driverless car should next act, after striking the animal. I think we can all agree that backing up or turning around on a road, whether during daytime or nighttime, bodes for potential driving risks and we need to ponder how well the AI could handle this.

There might also be damage done to the driverless car. Suppose that the cameras or radar or LIDAR being used as key sensory devices for the driving task are now out of commission, having been hit when the car struck the animal, or worse still maybe the sensors are now flaky and unreliable, yet perhaps the AI doesn't realize so (it might try to continue driving, even though it is now getting sketchy images or hazy data).

Conclusion

I've purposely chosen what seems on the surface to be a rather unique and unusual edge case to illustrate the boundaries of what AI systems need to be able to deal with when driving on our roadways.

I'd like to point out though that this is not quite that extraordinary per se, since as mentioned there are 20,000 deer strikes each year in California and some additional number of strikes involving wild pigs, elk, and other creatures. Taking the perspective of hitting any kind of animals, including domesticated dogs and cats, some reports suggest that our beloved pets are being killed in the millions nationwide each year by car strikes, thus the corner or edge is not really that remote of a possibility.

Plus, when this (assumed) edge case occurs, it can be traumatizing for all, including the passengers in the driverless car, nearby human drivers in other cars, pedestrians that might be nearby, and so on. An AI system that just ignores what happened or that becomes confounded as to what to do, it's not a good thing.

Keep your eye on those so-called edge or corner case aspects of autonomous cars and realize that the AI doesn't have common-sense reasoning and won't just magically "know" how to deal with some unusual or even some rather commonplace driving circumstances.

I'll be pondering all of this when I go have lunch today with a friend that mumbled something about having cooked some fresh meat that he found yesterday.

CHAPTER 3
SAFE DRIVER CITIES
AND
AI SELF-DRIVING CARS

CHAPTER 3

SAFE DRIVER CITIES
AND
AI SELF-DRIVING CARS

The annual ranking of the top cities in the United States for having the "safest" drivers has been recently published by Allstate Insurance, the chronicler of the *America's Best Driver's Report*.

I'm sure that you want to know who is the best and also who is the worst.

Of the 200 cities listed, the "best" five in terms of being at the top of the list were:

- Brownsville, TX (ranked in position 1)

- Boise, ID (ranked in position 2)

- Huntsville, AL (ranked in position 3)

- Kansas City, KS (ranked in position 4)

- Laredo, TX (ranked in position 5)

Of the 200 cities listed, the "worst" in terms of ending at the final pole positions of 196 through 200 were:

- Glendale, CA (ranked in position 196)

- Worcester, MA (ranked in position 197)

- Boston, MA (ranked in position 198)

- Washington D.C. (ranked in position 199)

- Baltimore, MD (ranked at the bottom of the listing, 200th place)

Some people glance at the list to see where their particular city has landed. Some use the list to be extra cautious when driving in the cities that are toward the latter portion of the list. There are some that find the list amusing and perhaps goad their friends or colleagues, bragging when their city is above or below the home city of the braggard.

In fact, there are people that relish being considered in the lower ranks, claiming that it shows just how good a driver they must be that they have to contend with so many other rotten drivers in their own city.

Generally, drivers tend to think they are good at driving, and don't see themselves as being a bad or lousy driver, instead believing that it is everyone else around them that are the culprit miscreant drivers.

It might be worthwhile to take a moment and reflect upon how the listing was derived. I say this because I've mentioned previously the importance of always scrutinizing various research studies about drivers and driving. You need to make sure that the headlines about a study can match adequately to the substance of the study.

Besides analyzing this study, I'll toss another twist into the mix, let's consider how this ranking might change in an era of self-driving driverless cars.

You might be surprised to see how the listing could change.

Unpacking The Existing Study

If you were trying to figure out which cities in the United States has the "safest" drivers, what method or approach would you use?

There are lots of ways you might conduct such a study.

In the case of the Allstate Insurance approach, they opted to use their own automobile claims data and examined principally the number of years between collisions, as reported via their claims database. According to Allstate, their automobile policies represent about 10% of all U.S. automobile policies.

It doesn't seem to be reported how the 10% of their U.S. automobile polices is spread across the United States, and it could be that some cities and states are over or underrepresented, thus, the resulting claims data could be statistically skewed. Also, the claims themselves might be skewed in terms of perhaps more so claims being reported or less claims being reported for that 10% of the U.S. automobile policies in comparison to the nationwide total of all automobile policies. And so on.

I'm not going to argue the point and instead will agree to stipulate that presumably their data is representative across the United States, especially since the ranking is not an especially life-or-death matter and not so crucial that we'd want to be more assured about its representative nature.

Likewise, you could have qualms about using the metric of the number of years between reported collisions. Reportedly, their data suggests that the average driver in these top ranked cities gets into a collision every 15 years, while the overall national average is every 10.57 years. That's an important point in that it implies there are presumably a lot more cities beyond this list of 200 that are increasingly worse, meaning they are tending toward a higher frequency of collisions.

To clarify, the longer the years interval, the better, since it implies that you are having less frequent collisions. Thus, collisions every 15 years is better than collisions every 10.57 years.

You might right away be concerned that the population size of a given city would have a potentially dramatic impact on the number of collisions per year. If you have a lesser population, and if this suggests you have a lesser number of licensed drivers, perhaps there is a lessened chance of getting into collisions, simply because there are less driving efforts underway.

Or, maybe you have an equal number of drivers, but your city is compacted and the drivers tend to be driving closely to each other, maybe leading to more collisions than otherwise in a more spread-out locale.

You could also bring up that the roadways of the city are a factor. If you live in a city that might have cruddy roadways, possibly designed during the horse and buggy era, or that your city is not keeping up to par, it could tend toward more collisions, and somewhat hiddenly impact the driving related stats.

Yes, all of those aforementioned elements can come to play.

It is for those and other such bona fide reasons that you should take any such listing of "safest drivers" with a grain of salt.

I'll say this, at least however the list has been prepared, given any list that is genuinely sincere, it sheds light and attention on the importance of us all being safer drivers. That's worthy for any methodological reservations as it brings drivers to the realization that they ought to be taking driving seriously and not let themselves become complacent in the driving task.

Era Of Self-Driving Driverless Cars

Now for the icing on the cake, as it were.

I had mentioned that the list might change once self-driving driverless cars become prevalent.

The smarmy answer to how the list would change is that presumably in a fully autonomous car world there would be no collisions ever again, and the list would no longer have any significance. You would merely say that all cities are equal in driving safety. No need to craft a list of that.

In essence, if you got into an autonomous car in Brownsville, Texas (ranked on the existing list as the safest driving city), you would have the same exact safety as you would while riding in an autonomous car while in Baltimore, Maryland (ranked at the bottom of the existing list of 200 cities). Not only would the safety be the same, this Utopian viewpoint is that your safety is guaranteed, meaning you have zero chance of getting into a collision.

Well, I've been repeatedly trying to debunk this notion of so-called zero fatalities and zero incidents due to autonomous cars that some pundits keep trying to parlay onto the media. It is a dreamland scenario that won't happen.

Cars are still cars, even when they are an autonomous car. Tires will still blowout. Car mechanical parts will still breakdown. The complex software and systems of an autonomous car will have bugs or errors, along with being subject to real-time failures and sensory issues. Pedestrians will still jump in front of a moving car, which no matter how good an autonomous car might be, it cannot overcome the physics when there is insufficient time to stop.

Plus, the Utopian perspective seems to assume that we'll have all and only self-driving driverless cars on our roadways. That's a quite debatable contention.

We have 250 million conventional cars today in the United States alone. Economically, those cars are not going to be switched out overnight to make way for autonomous cars. Thus, for a long time, we are likely to have human driven cars mixing with driverless cars. Collisions will happen, either because the driverless car failed to anticipate the action of a human driver, or a human driver has run into or bumped against a driverless car.

Conclusion

Back to the cities ranking, we can anticipate that there will be a gradual adoption and spread of autonomous cars and this emergence will not happen necessarily uniformly across the face of the country.

Assuming that driverless cars are likely to be used for ridesharing and acting as a money maker for some owner, perhaps in a fleet of autonomous cars by an automaker or a ridesharing firm, you need to consider where those driverless cars will be placed.

Would you put your limited supply of autonomous cars in a smaller city like Brownsville (population of around 180,000) or a larger city like Baltimore (population around 612,000)?

Everything else being equal, you'd probably be more likely to make more money in the higher populated areas, assuming that the populace embraces riding in autonomous cars.

If you believe that AI-run driverless cars will tend to be safer "drivers" than human drivers, you then need to start exploring the proportion of autonomous cars that will be appearing in any given city over time. It could be that as the proportion of autonomous cars versus human drivers rises in say Baltimore, the safety as based on years between collisions goes up (that's good), and might surpass Brownsville, assuming that Brownsville remains predominantly human driven focused.

The trickle effect of autonomous car adoption might be a shot in the arm for any city that perchance is more attractive for those that are deploying driverless cars, boosting the safety driving record in that city, even while human drivers are still on the roads there.

A counter argument that some make is that the human drivers might resent or detest their driverless brethren autonomous cars and allow a new kind of road rage to emerge, whereby the human driver purposely seeks to strike or cut-off driverless cars. If that scenario were to actually occur, it would potentially suggest that any such city would actually arrive at a worse "safety driving" record due to the advent of autonomous cars in their locale.

Though there have admittedly been some minor incidents and skirmishes already of human drivers attempting to bully driverless cars, I believe it is a stretch of the imagination to assert that human drivers will openly attempt to ram or get into collisions with driverless cars on any widespread basis, especially once the novelty of being near an autonomous car wears off.

I'm suggesting that human drivers will eventually take it for granted that there are driverless cars in the traffic with them.

CHAPTER 4

TAILGATE PARTIES
AND
AI SELF-DRIVING CARS

CHAPTER 4

TAILGATE PARTIES AND
AI SELF-DRIVING CARS

Tailgate parties.

According to the illustrious Homer Simpson, tailgate parties constitute the pinnacle of human achievement (a memorable statement made in the *Any Given Sundance* episode of The Simpsons).

Historically, tailgate parties were believed to have been started as part of college football attendance, offering a pre-game opportunity for some camaraderie and spirited fun among fans of the teams playing football.

Cars would fill into a parking lot adjacent to the stadium housing an upcoming game, drivers and their passengers would open-up the tailgates of their respective cars and then use the handy tailgate as a platform to get a party going.

I'll next describe salient aspects about tailgate parties, and then discuss a rather intriguing question, namely whether tailgate parties will continue to exist in an era of self-driving driverless cars.

Let's unpack the topic.

Some Background About Tailgate Parties

For those of you not familiar with what a tailgate is, it's that thing on station wagons that would fold down at the back of the vehicle, which admittedly doesn't have the same popularity as it once did, though having an actual tailgate per se is not a specific requirement to partake in tailgating. Nowadays, you can use the trunk space of your car, or the open back area of your SUV, or the actual tailgate of your pick-up truck, and so on.

Tailgating has generally morphed into the overall notion of assembling in a parking lot, prior to a sporting event, and standing or sitting around near the backs of the parked vehicles, doing so to have food and drink, along with sharing in the excitement and spirit of being together for the upcoming game.

In fact, it doesn't have to be a sporting event at all. Believe it or not, some people undertake tailgate parties for weddings, birthday celebrations, and a slew of other special occasions.

Anyone that hasn't been to tailgate party might wonder what takes place at these proceedings.

Well, you might sit on the tailgate and carryon banter with your fellow attendees. You might toss around a football or play lighthearted games of cornhole, horseshoes, ladder golf, or participate in the ever-present sport of beer pong. Be forewarned that some tailgaters are bound to get lit (today's parlance for becoming intoxicated).

Surprisingly, you (usually) would even be willing to interact civilly with tailgaters that were supporting the opposing team (though this custom seems sadly to be eroding). Whereas you'd normally expect instant fisticuffs among fans of opposing teams, it used to be considered untoward to bicker and fight when everyone was there at the tailgate party for presumably joyous reasons.

Refreshments including soda and alcohol might be placed onto the tailgate. Food might be placed onto the tailgate too, though the proper etiquette for true tailgaters is to cook or grill your food while tailgating, rather than having prepared the food beforehand.

The act of tailgating for some events will at times overshadow the event itself.

Some people come to tailgate and then do not attend directly the sporting event that was the reason to presumably have the tailgating to begin with. They stay in the parking lot and just continue to party while the game is underway.

And, due to the advent of electronics and the internet, in many cases the devoted tailgaters can watch the entire game on a TV that's plugged into the electrical power of their car.

Plus, it could be that your comfort level might be better by remaining in the tailgating area anyway, rather than having to squeeze into tightly packed stadium seats and only getting a limited view of the game due to a stadium steel post in front of you, or maybe have your view blocked as a result of some frantic fans that refuse to sit down throughout the game.

Curiously, some don't pay any attention to the game and either head home or stay to just party until the stadium security says that the parking lot must be emptied.

It turns out that tailgating is mainly an American kind of activity, shaped due to our culture and to some degree perhaps our geography.

We tend to have large parking lots surrounding our sports stadiums, which some countries don't do, along with generally good weather (not always, of course), and we have a car-focused or one might say car maniac mindset that spurs us to do nearly anything to involve our automobiles into our daily lives.

Advent Of Self-Driving Cars

Will any of the tailgating aspects change as a result of the advent of self-driving driverless cars?

Before we can explore the question, it is important to clarify that I am referring to fully autonomous cars, often considered at a Level 4 or Level 5.

A true self-driving driverless car is one that the AI is completely driving the car and there is no human driving involved. In contrast, a Level 2 or Level 3 car is known as a semi-autonomous car, meaning that there must be a human driver present and that the automation and the human driver are co-sharing the driving task.

All in all, I don't anticipate much of a change in tailgating as the emergence of Level 3 cars continues to occur. These more advanced semi-autonomous cars are still pretty much the same as today's cars, requiring a human driver for the driving act.

But I do think that tailgating will change in an era of fully autonomous cars, the ones that have no human driver and only an AI system doing the driving.

Your first thought might be that a car is a car, so why should tailgating change due to a car that is human driven versus one that is driven by AI.

Yes, you are certainly right that a car is still a car. The fully autonomous cars can just as readily have a tailgate or be used in a tailgating activity.

Here's the rub.

Some pundits argue that true self-driving driverless cars are going to be utilized nearly non-stop 24x7, driving around endlessly, since the AI will never get tired of driving and the autonomous car can be continually kept in service (other than for say charging the car, or for fixing any breakdowns).

Furthermore, the endlessly driving autonomous car can be making money, presumably, during each moment that it is driving around. If you put the autonomous car into a ridesharing network and let people pay to use it, you've got yourself a (hopefully) big bucks money maker.

We don't yet know whether the economics of autonomous cars is going to indeed make this into a heaven-sent flow of cash, but many believe it will.

Okay, if you go along with that key premise, I can now share with you why the tailgate activities of the future might evaporate.

It would seemingly make no sense to park your fully autonomous car in a stadium parking lot for several hours, doing nothing other than looking pretty, meanwhile it is not making any money as a result of providing people with rides.

Sure, you could "eat" the cost yourself and decide that you'll pay to have the driverless car parked for hours at a time. That's going to increase the costs of tailgating.

Some believe that all autonomous cars are going to be owned by large firms that put the driverless cars into ridesharing fleets. Thus, if you used a driverless car to get to the stadium, it is going to zip along to the next paying passenger and not stay there at the stadium, unless as I've mentioned you opt to continue paying for a fully autonomous car that's a multi-ton paperweight for tailgating purposes.

I've said many times that I believe there will be individual ownership of autonomous cars, creating a sizable cottage industry of private owners that decide to use their driverless cars to get to work and then the rest of the day their autonomous car earns them dough by ridesharing.

If I'm right about that private ownership aspect, the problem remains that you would be losing the opportunity of ridesharing out your autonomous car during the tailgating activity.

Maybe that would be Okay for you, and you might consider it as part of your downtime for your self-driving car, but it won't be the same as parking your today's conventional car that otherwise wasn't going anywhere anyhow and was not a money maker.

More About Tailgating And Self-Driving Cars

You could argue that maybe a tailgating party doesn't need cars.

Perhaps have autonomous cars drop-off the tailgating attendees, they unload their barbeques and other tailgating accouterments, and they party without any parked cars.

I think that's called a picnic.

And, consider another facet about the advent of self-driving cars that's likely to change our world, dealing with the role and placement of parking lots.

There are pundits that claim we will alter the nature and locations of our parking lots once autonomous cars become prevalent. The logic is that you won't need to have parking spaces anymore that are near to where humans want to be, since the driverless cars can simply drop-off its passengers and then go someplace else to park, perhaps a distant place.

Of course, in theory the self-driving car shouldn't be parked for very long.

Anyone that owns an autonomous car will be desirous of minimizing the parking time and maximizing the in-motion customer paying time. Complex scheduling models will be developed that attempt to figure out whether it is better to keep a self-driving car going and going, aiming to be in the right place when a ridesharing request arises, versus being parked someplace and waiting for a ridesharing request.

For stadiums that host sporting events, they might decide to do away with the large-scale parking lots that surround the stadium.

Those massive parking lots aren't much of a money maker and usually exist mainly so that customers will come to the stadium and buy tickets to see the game, plus buy loads of the merchandise and food that's available in the stadium (that's usually where the profit for the stadium comes from).

It is quite conceivable that stadiums will do away with those massive parking lots, perhaps turning the space into something more money making such as condos or retail space. They could do so without fear of losing customers because by-and-large those coming to the stadium will be riding in an autonomous car that do a drop-off and don't hang around like today's conventional cars do.

Conclusion

I know it seems somewhat sad that I've now suggested that having parked autonomous cars is seemingly unlikely, knocking out a key cornerstone of tailgating parties, and I've also now made the point that there might not be any parking lots in which to undertake a tailgating effort, which is another vital cornerstone for tailgate revelry extravaganzas.

A crying shame.

Before you cry too much into your tailgating beer, let's see if we can find a means to keep tailgates alive.

In our streaming online world, how are stadiums going to inspire people to leave their homes and come to a stadium to watch an event?

Some assert that there is a shared experience that one gets by attending a sporting event in-person, and for which cannot be matched by simply watching it on your smartphone or TV at home.

Suppose stadiums decide that an important way to keep people coming to the stadium will be to provide a tailgating experience.

One trick would be to buy a bunch of outdated conventional cars and park them in the parking lot, sitting there for keeps. Those attending a sporting event at the stadium could reserve a specific parked car as their favorite one to tailgate with.

This might be a crucial attractor to keep people coming to the stadium.

The stadium might also try to make extra money by providing barbeques that are setup and ready to be used, possibly even catering your tailgating activity for you. I realize this seems antithetic to the existing tradition, but I believe that some of the tailgating facets are malleable and people might welcome having the tailgate effort become essentially "hassle free" for them.

One final point that might make you feel better about the future of tailgating.

Suppose that the cost of using autonomous cars drops so low that it is nearly trivial to rideshare in one. This would presumably be a boon for mobility.

It would also suggest that you could indeed use an autonomous car for hours at a time as a parked paperweight. If it was a relative pittance in cost, you would consider it the equivalent of the cost for the drinks and food that you bring to the tailgating activity.

There's an added bonus too about the use of autonomous cars for tailgating.

Most agree that self-driving driverless cars will be outfitted with V2V (vehicle-to-vehicle) electronic communications. This will allow the AI of one driverless car to communicate with the AI of another self-driving car, sharing roadway tips and insights, such as that debris might be up ahead on a freeway or that the traffic is snarled at the upcoming corner.

When parked for a tailgating party, imagine that the autonomous cars could communicate with each other. You might have them all honk their horns to the tune of your football team's anthem. Or, maybe turn on and off the headlights each time that your team scores a touchdown.

Is that an added thrill for tailgating, or maybe it seems peculiar, but in any case the notion is that perhaps tailgating will remain as strong as ever, and you'll be able to enjoy some great food, drink, and festive partying even in an era of true self-driving driverless cars.

I'll drink to that.

CHAPTER 5
TESLA'S AI CHIPS
AND AI SELF-DRIVING CARS

CHAPTER 5

TESLA'S AI CHIPS AND
AI SELF-DRIVING CARS

Let's jump right into the topic.

I am sick and tired of the breathless and misleading media reporting about Tesla's new AI chips that are supposed to help achieve Tesla's (hoped for) FSD or Full Self-Driving driverless car capability.

It's a glorification that inadvertently overstates the facts.

Before I explore the basis for this exasperating sense of qualm and outright concern about the reporting, let me clarify that the custom AI chips devised by the Tesla engineers are certainly admirable, and the computer hardware design team deserves to be proud of what they have done.

Kudos for their impressive work.

But such an acknowledgement does not also suggest that they have somehow achieved a marvel in AI, and nor does it mean they have miraculously solved the real-world problem of how to attain a true self-driving driverless car.

Not by a long shot.

And yet many in the media seem to think so, and at times have implied in a wide-eyed gasping way that Tesla's new computer processors have seemingly gone beyond this world and reached a nirvana of finally getting us to fully autonomous cars.

It's just not the case.

Hamburger Analogy Explains Disconnect

You might be wondering why those media reporters are getting it wrong.

For some media pundits, they don't seem to know how to differentiate between what they see and hear about these new processors versus what has actually been accomplished.

Perhaps it is due to a lack of understanding about what they are looking at and hearing about.

Suppose you didn't know much about hamburgers and tended to always get the simplest burger on the menu, perhaps a kid's meal version of a burger that was sparse and low-end.

If someone showed you a new adult-sized hamburger that had double the number of patties and included plentiful layers of pickles, lettuce, tomatoes, and onions, you might run to the hills and declare that a breakthrough in burgers had just taken place.

Incredible, amazing, mesmerizing, you might declare in your writeup about the new hamburger.

Meanwhile, anyone that really knew about burgers would know that there are other equivalent double patty burgers already available in the marketplace.

And, would know that there are even triple patty burgers.

Plus, would know that there are burgers with bacon, and some with a fried egg on top, all of which in various ways might eclipse this other new burger.

As such, I'd like to help out by explaining why the Tesla AI chips are interesting and worthy to consider, yet also properly depict the new hardware into an appropriate context that correctly establishes what it is and what it is not in terms of arriving at a true self-driving car.

Time to unpack the matter.

Important Context About AI Chips

First, let's clarify what an AI chip consists of.

This will be worth knowing, though maybe a bit wonky, as it directly pertains to the matter at-hand.

A conventional computer contains a core processor or chip that does the systems work when you invoke your word processor or spreadsheets or are loading and running an app that keeps track of your diet and trying to wean yourself away from eating too many hamburgers (yes, I've mentioned hamburgers once again!).

In addition, most modern computers also have GPU's, Graphical Processing Units, an additional set of processors or chip that aid the core processor by taking on the task of displaying visual graphics and animation that you might see on the screen of your device such as on the display of a desktop PC, a laptop or a smartphone.

To use computers for Machine Learning (ML) or Deep Learning (DL), it was realized that rather than necessarily using the normal core processors of a computer to do so, the GPU's actually tended to be better suited for the ML or DL tasks.

This is essentially due to the aspect that by-and-large the implementation of artificial neural networks in today's computers is really a large-sized numeric and linear algebra kind of affair. GPU's are generally structured and devised for that kind of numeric mashing.

AI developers that rely upon ML/DL computer-based neural networks fell in love with GPU's, utilizing GPU's for something not particularly originally envisioned but that happens to be a good marriage anyway.

Once it became apparent that having souped-up GPU's would help advance today's kind of AI, the chip developers realized that it could be a huge market potential for their processors and therefore merited their tweaking the GPU designs to more closely fit to the ML/DL task.

Tesla had opted to use off-the-shelf specialized GPU chips made by NVIDIA, doing so for the Tesla in-car on-board processing efforts of the Tesla version of ADAS (Advanced Driver Assistance System), including and especially for their so-called Tesla AutoPilot (a naming that has generated controversy for being misleading about the actual driverless functionality to-date available in their so-equipped "FSD" cars).

In April of this year, Elon Musk and his team proudly unveiled a set of proprietary AI chips that were secretly developed in-house by Tesla (rumors about the effort had been floating for quite a while), and the idea was that the new chips would replace the use of the Tesla on-board in-car NVIDIA processors.

This was a key portion of the Investor Autonomy Day event that Tesla used as a forum for announcing the future plans of their hoped-for someday self-driving driverless capability.

Subsequently, in August, a presentation was made by Tesla engineers depicting some additional details about their custom-designed chips, doing so at the annual Hot Chips conference sponsored by the IEEE and focusing on high performance computer processors.

As such, media interest in reporting about the Tesla AI chips was reinvigorated recently by the symposium and led to what I am asserting consists of a furtherance of overstated and wrongly glorified statements being made about the matter.

One additional important point -- most people refer to these kinds of processors as "AI chips," which I'll do too for ease of discussion herein, but please do not be lulled into believing that these specialized processors are actually fulfilling the long-sought goal of being able to have Artificial Intelligence in all of its intended facets.

At best, these chips or processors are simulating relatively shallow mathematically inspired aspects of what might be called neural networks, but it isn't at all anything akin to a human brain. There isn't any human-like reasoning or common-sense capability involved in these chips. They are merely computationally enhanced numeric calculating devices.

Brouhaha About Tesla's New Chips

Okay, the bottom-line is that Tesla opted to replace the NVIDIA chips and did so by designing and now deploying their own Tesla-designed chips (the chips are being manufactured for Tesla by Samsung).

Let's now consider a myriad of vital questions about the matter.

- Did it make sense for Tesla to have gone on its own to make specialized chips, or would they have been better off to continue using someone else's off-the-shelf specialized chips?

- On a comparison basis, how are the Tesla custom chips different or the same as off-the-shelf specialized chips that do roughly the same thing?

- And so on.

Here's my answers as formulated in a brief way to give you the overall skinny (there's a lot more detail that I could provide, but I'm trying to keep this analysis short-and-sweet).

My thoughts are:

- ***Hardware-Only Focus***

It is crucial to realize that discussing these AI chips is only a small part of a bigger picture, since the chips are a hardware-only focused element.

You need software, really good software, in order to arrive at a true self-driving car.

Suppose someone comes out with a new smartphone that is incompatible with the thousands upon thousands of apps in the marketplace. Even if the smartphone is superfast, you have the rather more daunting issue that there aren't any apps for the new hardware.

Media salivating over the Tesla AI chips is missing the boat on asking about the software needed to arrive at driverless capabilities.

I'm not saying that having good hardware is not important, it is, but I think we all know now that hardware is only part of the battle.

The software to do true AI self-driving is the 500-pound gorilla.

- ***Force-fit Of Design***

If you were going to design a new AI chip, one approach would be to sit down and come up with all of the vital things you'd like to have the chip do. You would blue sky it, starting with a blank sheet, aiming to stretch the boundaries as much as feasible.

For Tesla, the hardware engineers were actually handed a circumstance that imposed a lot of severe constraints on what they could devise.

They had to keep the electrical power consumption within a boundary dictated by the prior designs of the Tesla cars, otherwise it would mean that the Tesla cars already in the marketplace would have to undergo a major retrofit to allow for a more power hungry set of processors. That would be costly and economically infeasible. Thus, right away the new AI chip would be bounded by how much power it could consume.

The new processors would have to fit into the physical space as already set aside on existing Tesla cars, meaning that the size and shape of the on-board system boards and computer box would have to abide by a strict "form factor."

Etc.

This is the downside of being the first into a market.

You come out with a product, it gains some success, and so you need to then try to advance the product as the marketplace evolves, yet you are also somewhat trapped by needing to be backward compatible with what you already did.

Those that come along after you've got your product underway have the latitude of not being trapped by what came before and can oftentimes out-perform by having a blank slate to work with.

Indeed, though more so service oriented than product oriented, some would assert that the Uber and Lyft ridesharing phenomena happened because they ignored existing constraints faced by taxi's and cabs, allowing these ridesharing upstarts to eclipse those that were hampered by the past (rightfully or wrongly so).

Being first in something is not necessarily always the best, and sometimes those that come along later on can move in a more agile way.

- ### *Improper Comparisons*

One of my biggest beefs about the media reporting has been the willingness to fall into a misleading and improper comparison of the Tesla AI chips to other chips.

I'll use the hamburgers again.

After coming out with a double patty burger, suppose the media gushed about how much better it is than the kid's meal single-patty burger.

Seems logical.

Logical but misleading if there are other double patty burgers already in existence.

Comparing the new with the old is not especially helpful, though it sounds exciting when you do so, and instead the comparison should be with what else exists in the marketplace.

Here's what I mean.

Most keep saying that the Tesla AI chips are many times faster than the prior-used NVIDIA chips (though they ought to be comparing to NVIDIA's other newer chips), implying that Tesla made a breathtaking breakthrough in this kind of technology, often quoting the number of trillions of operations per second, known as TOPS.

It's like comparing the double-patty against a single-patty, when you should be comparing the new double-patty against other double patties.

I won't bore you with the details herein, but suffice to say that the Tesla AI chips TOPS performance is either on par with other alternatives, or in some ways less so, and in other way better than, but it is not a hit-it-out-of-the-ballpark revelation.

Stop making the false and inappropriate comparisons between the Tesla AI chips and the prior-used NVIDIA chips, it doesn't make sense, it is misleading to the public, it is unfair to NVIDIA, and it really shows ignorance about the topic.

Another pet peeve is the tossing around of big numbers to impress the non-initiated, such as the media touting that the Tesla AI chips consist of 6 billion transistors.

On my gosh, 6 billion seems like such a large number and implies something gargantuan. Well, there are GPU's that already have 20 billion transistors. I'm not denigrating the 6 billion, and only trying to point out that those quoting the 6 billion do so without offering any viable context and therefore imply something that isn't really the case.

Note, for you hardware types, I know and you know that trying to make a comparison by the number of transistors is a rather myopic exercise anyway since it can be an apples-to-apples or an apple-to-oranges kind of comparison, depending upon what the chip is designed to do.

- **First Gen Is Dicey**

Anybody that knows anything about chip design can tell you that the first generation of a newly devised chip is oftentimes a rocky road.

There can be a slew of hidden errors or bugs (if you prefer, we can be gentler in our terminology and refer to those aspects as quirks or the proverbial tongue-in-cheek "hidden features").

Like the first version of any new product, the odds are that it will take a shakeout period to ferret out what might be amiss.

In the case of chips, since it is encased in silicon and not readily changeable, there are sometimes software patches used to deal with hardware issues, and then in later versions of the chip you might make the needed hardware alterations and improvements.

This brings up the point that by Tesla choosing to make its own AI chips, rather than using an off-the-shelf approach, it puts Tesla into the unenviable position of having a first gen and needing to figure out on-their-own whatever guffaws those new chips might have.

Typically, an off-the-shelf commercially available chip is going to have not just the original maker looking at it and will have those that are buying and incorporating the processor into their systems looking at it too. The more eyes, the better.

The Tesla proprietary chips are presumably only being scrutinized and tested by Tesla alone.

- ***Proprietary Chip Woes***

Using your own self-designed chips has a lot of other considerations worth noting.

At Tesla, there would have been a significant cost and attention that was devoted toward devising the AI chips.

Was that cost worth it?

Was the diverted attention that might have gone to other matters a lost opportunity cost?

Plus, Tesla not only had to bear the original design cost, they will have to bear the ongoing cost to presumably upgrade and improve the chip over time.

This is not a one-time only kind of matter.

It would seem unlikely and unwise for Tesla to sit on this chip and not advance it, which as you likely know, the advances in AI chips are moving at lightening-like paces.

There are also the labor pool considerations too.

Having a proprietary chip usually means that you have to grow your own specialists to be able to develop the specialized software for it. You cannot just find those specialists in the marketplace per se, since they won't know your proprietary stuff, whereas when you use a commercial off-the-shelf chip, the odds are that you can find labor for it since there is an ecosystem surrounding the off-the-shelf processor.

I am not saying that Tesla was mistaken to go the proprietary route, and only time will tell whether it was a worthwhile bet.

By having their own chip, they can potentially control their own destiny and not be dependent upon an off-the-shelf chip made by someone else, and not be forced into the path of the off-the-shelf chip maker.

It's a calculated gamble and a trade-off.

From a cost perspective, it might or might not be a sensible approach, and those that keep trying to imply that the proprietary chip is a lesser cost strategy are likely not including the full set of costs involved.

Be wary of those that do off-the-cuff cost claims.

- **Redundancy Assertions**

There has been media excitement about how the Tesla AI chips supposedly have a robust redundancy capability, which certainly is essential for a real-time system that involves the life-and-death aspects of driving a car.

So far, the scant details revealed seemed to be that there are two identical AI chips running in parallel and if one of the chips disagrees with the other chip that the current assessment of the driving situation and planned next step is discarded, allowing for the next "frame" to be captured and analyzed.

On the surface, this might seem dandy to those that haven't developed fault-tolerant real-time systems before.

If you somehow assume that one of the chips maybe had a hiccup and thus led to the identical chips disagreeing with each other, this oddball quirky moment is (presumably) thankfully realized by the aspect that the two chips don't agree, and the ball is punted further down-the-field, so to speak.

I'm certainly hopeful that there is a lot more to this than what has been portrayed in the media.

Suppose the oddball quirk isn't just a single momentary fluke, and instead recurs.

Does this mean that both chips are going to continually disagree and therefore presumably keep postponing the act of making a driving decision? If you were driving a car, and you kept postponing making a driving decision, imagine if that decision involved whether or not to swerve to avoid that gasoline tanker sitting in the road ahead.

Not making a decision is not necessarily the best driving strategy.

Another facet is the idea that both chips have to agree.

Well, suppose that both chips make a bad decision, which could happen, and since they are identical and presumably going to agree, you then have a reinforced bad decision as based simply on the aspect that both agreed to it.

This is why oftentimes you purposely create a second (or third) redundant system that is separate and not identical, trying to overcome the chances of a flaw inside a simple repeated or duplicated system.

Yet another facet is the need for a kind of self-awareness capability, namely that if the two chips disagree, why did they disagree?

And, equally or maybe more importantly, what can be learned via the disagreement that might improve their ability to jointly agree when they perhaps shouldn't be disagreeing.

I can go on-and-on (see my articles on fault tolerance for AI self-driving cars, and my piece too about arguing machines and autonomous cars).

I think you get the gist that there's a lot more to proper redundancy and so the media that touts how Tesla has opted to do so is really offering an ill-informed opinion without any proper basis to make the assertion that it is robust.

It might be, and I'm not saying that it isn't, and only saying that the media shouldn't be alluding to something that we don't know has legs or not.

Conclusion

Some have said that it is a gutsy move by Tesla to have gone the self-designed custom chip route for their self-driving car capabilities.

Was it a smart and business savvy choice?

Was it a vanity decision?

Will it turnout to be their best decision or their worst decision?

Overall, it is a bet-the-company kind of gamble, since their ability to achieve true self-driving driverless cars rides on that decision.

You might say they've cashed all their chips in on these new AI chips.

CHAPTER 6

ELITES-ONLY AND
AI SELF-DRIVING CARS

CHAPTER 6

ELITES-ONLY AND
AI SELF-DRIVING CARS

Via the advent of true self-driving driverless cars, many hope and assume that we are heading toward mobility-for-all.

The notion and belief is that with commonly and readily available car transportation, being undertaken by AI driving systems that won't tire out and that will ensure that cars are around 24x7 and ready to go, the opportunity for everyone to make use of mobility will finally become a reality.

This includes those today that are at a mobility disadvantage, a segment of society that oftentimes gets little attention and nor support for their mobility needs.

But not all prognosticators agree that we will indeed achieve mobility-for-all.

There are some that warn and fret that maybe autonomous cars are going to be mobility-for-the-few.

The somewhat bleaker scenario is that self-driving cars will turnout to be so expensive that only the elite will be able to afford to use these upcoming AI-based driverless cars.

Which will it be for self-driving cars, the shining light of mobility-for-all or the exclusive elitist mobility-for-the few?

Let's unpack the question and decide.

The Rise Of Elitism For Self-Driving Cars

Before we can closely examine the question, it is important to clarify that I am referring to fully autonomous cars, often considered at a Level 4 or Level 5.

A true self-driving driverless car is one that the AI is completely driving the car and there is no human driving involved. In contrast, a Level 2 or Level 3 car is known as a semi-autonomous car, meaning that there must be a human driver present and that the automation and the human driver are co-sharing the driving task.

All in all, during the emergence of Level 3 cars, I don't anticipate much of a change in car ownership and nor car usage. These more advanced semi-autonomous cars are still pretty much the same as today's cars, requiring a human driver for the driving act.

But I do think that car ownership and car usage will change in an era of fully autonomous cars, the ones that have no human driver and only an AI system doing the driving.

I'll start with the perspective that true self-driving cars will become the nearly exclusive use of the rich and famous, a viewpoint that many worry could readily occur.

How could that happen?

First, it could be that self-driving cars cost an arm and a leg to develop and field. If the cost of a driverless car is quite high, naturally it stands to reason that those that want to purchase such an AI-based car will need to pay a hefty price.

Presumably, only very wealthy people could afford those autonomous cars.

If you already have a collection of fancy cars, it would be a nice addition to include the latest self-driving car in your automotive menagerie.

Imagine yourself showcasing the driverless car in your mansion-equipped gargantuan garage or home automotive museum, letting friends and guests gawk and admire the sleek new form of transport.

Perhaps you'd go for a drive in your self-driving car, doing so without the need for your human chauffeur since the AI will be doing the driving. Cruising on the freeway, you instruct the AI to take you to the downtown area, letting everyday (commoner) pedestrians see what it is like to be inside a state-of-the-art car.

The special computer-controlled windows of the driverless car could be turned transparent or opaque, simply by your telling the AI to make use of the built-in feature accordingly.

As an aside, one predicted reaction to the possibility that only the wealthy will have self-driving cars is that people and society might somewhat rebel, either in subtle ways or more overt ways.

For example, as a pedestrian, suppose you know that the AI system of driverless cars has been programmed to never threaten a pedestrian in the roadway. Today's human drivers play a game of chicken with pedestrians, but in the future the driverless cars might simply concede the street to any jaywalker.

As such, if you perchance spy one of those fancy types coming down the street in their lavish self-driving car, you might purposely wander into the street, forcing the AI system to come to a halt, not necessarily entering into the street because you wanted to cross the street and only to disturb or disrupt that no-good high-and-mighty passenger in the driverless car.

Another rebellious act might involve human drivers that come near to a self-driving car while in traffic.

We already know that human drivers will sometimes exhibit road rage against other human drivers. The same road rage could be displayed toward self-driving cars. You might drive your car in front of a self-driving car and try to confuse it or confound the AI, doing so by undertaking tricky and risky maneuvers with your human driven car.

It could get ugly on our highways and streets if people resent the exclusive and glorified use of vaunted driverless cars.

A recent news item about how some wealthy Chinese drivers have behaved badly toward other drivers and pedestrians is maybe a preview of what could happen. The have's might become emboldened by their self-driving cars and use them in obnoxious ways, though presumably the AI system will be programmed to prevent untoward driving behavior, even if the entitled-minded passenger tries to command the AI to do inappropriate driving acts.

Well, there are some that doubt that individuals, even wealthy ones, will own self-driving cars, and instead we'll witness self-driving cars only being owned by large corporations, each such company commanding a massive fleet of driverless cars.

This perhaps makes sense in that the money to be made from self-driving cars could be based on large-scale ridesharing or ride-hailing activities.

Automobile makers or ride-sharing firms or pretty much any large company might decide to buy an entire herd of self-driving cars and put them each to work. Sure, the cost of those self-driving cars might be high, but the revenue and profit will be even higher.

And, when compared to human driven ridesharing services, the fleet owners will not have to deal with those pesky human drivers that might unionize or otherwise carp about driving and driving and driving (along with how much they are or are not getting paid to do the driving).

So, in this elitism scenario, self-driving cars will only be owned by big time firms and perhaps not even the well-to-do will have them.

This seems a bit outstretched though since you would think that a super-wealthy person could convince a fleet owner to sell them a self-driving car for their own private delight and ownership, of course only at the right sky-high price.

Another twist that some envision is that perhaps regulators will impose a law that says self-driving cars can only be owned in fleets.

Why would the government do such a thing?

Some suggest that regulators might be leery of individual ownership of self-driving cars in that the wealthy owners will potentially hog their driverless car and not allow it to be shared with others, denying the autonomous car from being available in a ridesharing pool.

It could be that the government opts to do a forced version of the democratization of self-driving cars, enacting rules and regulations that compel those that own driverless cars to make sure the driverless car becomes a form of public transportation.

This then takes us into the next overarching viewpoint, namely that maybe elitism won't reign over the advent of self-driving cars.

Elitism Won't Prevail Over Self-Driving Cars

Now that we've dug into the elitism perspective, let's consider what might mitigate or prevent an elitist world of self-driving cars from taking hold.

We would need to first distinguish the difference between car ownership and car usage.

As mentioned already, one scenario is that self-driving cars will be used primarily for ridesharing purposes.

Thus, it could be that only the wealthy or large firms could own self-driving cars, simply due to the affordability aspect, while at the same time those self-driving cars are readily available for public use by all.

This naturally raises the question of how much would the ridesharing fare be by those that wanted to use self-driving cars to take that trip to the grocery store or over to the hospital for their check-up.

Could the big-bucks owners make sufficient money by ridesharing out their expensive self-driving cars in a low-cost usage way?

Nobody knows.

One variant is that perhaps the ridesharing pricing might be structured or tiered in some fashion, maybe requiring by regulatory fiat that the fleet owners can only legally charge a certain amount for usage to certain segments of the population. Perhaps a movie star pays more to use a ridesharing self-driving car while a store clerk that needs a lift to work pays a much smaller price.

Could the open market economic mechanisms even bring about that kind of relative pricing, doing so without having to put in place governmental regulations?

Or, via marketplace capitalistic practices, suppose the competition is so fierce among the fleet owners of self-driving cars that they have essentially no choice but to keep their usage prices low.

Here's the logic.

Imagine if we today had a glut of human driven ridesharing cars, meaning that the number of available ridesharing cars swamped the area where you work or live. The moment you walk out of your house, you see dozens of ridesharing cars all cruising down your street. You have the pick of the litter, being able to log into a ridesharing network and have the ridesharing drivers bidding on imploring you to pick them.

In theory, such intense competition would bring down the prices.

Some believe that the same thing could happen with driverless cars.

It might be the case that driverless cars are manufactured like hotcakes. The next thing we all know, they are everywhere. The fleet owners are faced with a plentiful supply of self-driving cars, beyond what the demand for the use of self-driving cars seems to be.

Voila, self-driving cars are affordable for all.

Mobility-for-all reigns supreme.

Conclusion

I'm somewhat known for having a (some say) contrarian viewpoint about the ownership of self-driving cars, namely that I assert we'll have everyday folks that own driverless cars.

My claim is based on the important point that today's car ownership has little or nothing to do with trying to make money from your car, which some falsely are extending the same concept into the future.

Sure, those that rideshare with their privately-owned vehicle are aiming to make money via their car, but the preponderance of 250 million or so car owners in the United States merely use their car for private use and don't profit per se from their car ownership.

If you knew that you could make money by owning a self-driving car, which you might then also use for your personal purposes, wouldn't you be tempted to buy one?

Suppose tomorrow you could take your self-driving car to work, and while at the office for the next eight hours you had your driverless car roaming around as a ridesharing vehicle, bringing in dough.

You then use your self-driving car to get home at night, and while sleeping your driverless car is once again roaming and making money.

This would potentially provide you with a second income.

Those that say that self-driving cars will be costly to purchase are not considering the calculated ROI (return on investment) that might make shelling out big bucks worthwhile to buy one.

Yes, perhaps you need to get a hefty loan to buy a self-driving car, yet if the equation reveals that you'll profit by doing so, you would be foolhardy to not consider it.

I'm predicting that a cottage industry will arise, sitting alongside those large fleets of owned self-driving cars.

Anyway, I tend to believe that the elitism takeover of self-driving cars seems to be unlikely.

There might be a rough spot when self-driving cars are first becoming viable, during which there might be only wealthy related owners, almost like trying to be the first into a hot IPO, but once that era passes, I believe that the mobility-for-the-few will transform into the mobility-for-the-all.

Maybe I'm optimistic, and if so, I'm happy that I am.

CHAPTER 7

FOUR YEAR LIFECYCLE
AND AI SELF-DRIVING CARS

CHAPTER 7

FOUR YEAR LIFECYCLE AND AI SELF-DRIVING CARS

A recent news item about self-driving cars has been creating quite a flurry of debate due to the suggestion by a major automotive maker that driverless cars might only last about four years.

Some are shocked that autonomous cars might merely be usable for a scant four years at a time and then presumably end-up on the junk heap.

Let's unpack the matter and explore the ramifications of a presumed four-year life span for self-driving cars.

Life Span Of Cars

According to various stats about today's cars, the average age of a conventional car in the United States is estimated at 11.6 years old.

Some tend to use the 11.6 years or a rounded 12 years as a surrogate for how long a car lasts in the U.S, though this is somewhat problematic to do since the average age is not the endpoint of a car and encapsulates a range of ages of cars, including a slew of cars that were retired at a much younger age and those that hang-on to a much older age.

Indeed, one of the fastest growing segments of car ages is the group that is 16 years or older, amounting to an estimated 81 million such cars by the year 2021. Of those 81 million cars, around one-fourth are going to be more than 25 years old.

In short, cars are being kept around longer and longer.

When you buy a new car, the rule-of-thumb often quoted by auto makers is that the car should last about 8 years or 150,000 miles.

This is obviously a low-ball kind of posturing, trying to set expectations so that car buyers will be pleased if their cars last longer. One supposes it also perhaps gets buyers into the mental mode of considering buying their next car in about 8 years or so.

Continuing the effort to consider various stats about cars, Americans drive their cars for about 11,000 miles per year. If a new car is supposed to last for 150,000 miles, the math then suggests that at 11,000 miles per year you could drive the car for 14 years (that's 150,000 miles divided by 11,000 miles per year).

Of course, the average everyday driver is using their car for easy driving such as commuting to work and driving to the grocery store. Generally, you wouldn't expect the average driver to be putting many miles onto a car.

What about those that are pushing their cars to the limit and driving their cars in a much harsher manner?

Various published stats about ridesharing drivers such as Uber and Lyft suggest that they are amassing about 1,000 miles per week on their cars. If so, you could suggest that the number of miles per year would be approximately 50,000 miles. At the pace of 50,000 miles per year, presumably these on-the-go cars would only last about 3 years, based on the math of 150,000 miles divided by 50,000 miles per year.

In theory, this implies that a ridesharing car being used today will perhaps last about 3 years.

For self-driving cars, most would agree that a driverless car is going to be used in a similar ridesharing manner and be on-the-road quite a lot.

This seems sensible. To make as much money as possible with a driverless car, you would likely seek to maximize the use of it. Put it onto a ridesharing network and let it be used as much as people are willing to book it and pay to use it.

Without the cost and hassle of having to find and use a human driver for a driverless car, the AI will presumably be willing to drive a car whenever and however long is needed. As such, a true self-driving car is being touted as likely to be running 24x7.

In reality, you can't actually have a self-driving car that is always roaming around, since there needs to be time set aside for ongoing maintenance of the car, along with repairs, and some amount of time for fueling or recharging of the driverless car.

Overall, it would seem logical to postulate that a self-driving car will be used at least as much as today's human-driven ridesharing cars, plus a lot more so since the self-driving car is not limited by human driving constraints.

In short, if it is the case that today's ridesharing cars are hitting their boundaries at perhaps 3 to 5 years, you could reasonably extend that same thinking to driverless cars and assume therefore that self-driving cars might only last about four years.

The shock that a driverless car might only last four years is not quite as surprising when you consider that a true self-driving car is going to be pushed to its limits in terms of usage and be a ridesharing goldmine (presumably) that will undergo nearly continual driving time.

Factors Of Car Aging

There are three key factors that determine how long a car will last, namely:

- How the car was built
- How the car is used
- How the car is maintained

Let's consider how those key factors apply to self-driving cars.

In the case of today's early versions of what are intended to be driverless cars, by-and-large most of the auto makers are using a conventional car as the basis for their driverless car, rather than building an entirely new kind of car.

We will eventually see entirely new kinds of cars being made to fully leverage a driverless car capability, but for right now it is easier and more expedient to use a conventional car as the cornerstone for an autonomous car.

Therefore, for the foreseeable future, we can assume that the manner of how a driverless car was built is in keeping with how a conventional car is built, implying that the car itself will last as long as a conventional car might last.

In terms of the car usage, as already mentioned, a driverless car is going to get a lot more usage than the amount of driving by an average everyday driver and be used at least as much as today's ridesharing efforts. The usage is bound to be much higher.

The ongoing maintenance of a self-driving car will become vital to the owner of a driverless car.

I say this because any shortcomings on the maintenance would tend to mean that the driverless car will be in the shop and not be as available on the streets. The revenue stream from an always-on self-driving car will be a compelling reason for owners to make sure that their self-driving car is getting the proper amount of maintenance.

In that sense, the odds would seem to be the case that a driverless car will likely be better maintained than either an average everyday car or even today's ridesharing cars.

One additional element to consider for driverless cars consists of the add-ons for the sensory capabilities and the computer processing aspects. Those sensory devices such as cameras, radar, ultrasonic, LIDAR, and so on, need to be factored into the longevity of the overall car, and the same applies to the computer chips and memory on-board too.

Why Retire A Car

The decision to retire a car is based on a trade-off between trying to continue to pour money into a car that is breaking down and excessively costing money to keep afloat, versus ditching the car and opting to get a new or newer car instead.

Thus, when you look at how long a car will last, you are also silently considering the cost of a new or newer car.

We don't yet know what the cost of a driverless car is going to be.

If the cost is really high to purchase a self-driving car, you would presumably have greater incentive to try and keep a used self-driving car in sufficient working order.

There is also a safety element that comes to play in deciding whether to retire a self-driving car.

Suppose a driverless car that is being routinely maintained is as safe as a new self-driving car, but eventually the maintenance can only achieve so much in terms of ensuring that the driverless car remains as safe while driving on the roadways as would be a new or newer self-driving car.

The owner of the used self-driving car would need to ascertain whether the safety degradation means that the used driverless car needs to be retired.

Used Market For Self-Driving Cars

With conventional cars, an owner that first purchased a new car will likely sell the car after a while. We all realize that a conventional car might end-up being passed from one buyer to another over its life span.

Will there be an equivalent market for used self-driving cars?

You might be inclined to immediately suggest that once a self-driving car has reached some point of no longer being safe enough, it needs to be retired. We don't yet know, and no one has established what that safety juncture or threshold might be.

There could be a used self-driving car market that involved selling a used driverless car that was still within some bounds of being safe.

Suppose a driverless car owner that had used their self-driving car extensively in a downtown city setting opted to sell the autonomous car to someone that lived in a suburban community. The logic might be that the self-driving car no longer was sufficient for use in a stop-and-go traffic environment but might be viable in a less stressful suburban locale.

Overall, no one is especially thinking about used self-driving cars, which is admittedly a concern that is far away in the future and therefore not a topic looming over us today.

Retirement Of A Self-Driving Car

Other than becoming a used car, what else might happen to a self-driving car after its been in use for a while?

Some have wondered whether it might be feasible to convert a self-driving car into becoming a human-driven car, doing so to place the car into the used market for human-driven cars.

Well, it depends on how the self-driving car was originally made. If the self-driving car has all of the mechanical and electronic guts for human driving controls, you could presumably unplug the autonomy and revert the car into being a human driven car.

I would assert that this is very unlikely, and you won't see self-driving cars being transitioned into becoming human-driven cars.

All told, it would seem that once a self-driving car has reached its end of life, the vehicle would become scrapped.

If self-driving cars are being placed into the junk heap every four years, this raises the specter that we are going to have a lot of car junk piling up. For environmentalists, this is certainly disconcerting.

Generally, today's cars are relatively highly recyclable and reusable. Estimates suggest that around 80% of a car can be recycled or reused.

For driverless cars, assuming they are built like today's conventional cars, you would be able to potentially attain a similar recycled and reused parts percentage. The add-ons of the sensory devices and computer processors might be recyclable and reusable too, though this is not necessarily the case depending upon how the components were made.

Conclusion

There are critics that would be tempted to claim that the auto makers would adore having self-driving cars that last only four years.

Presumably, it would mean that the auto makers will be churning out new cars hand-over-fist, doing so to try and keep up with the demand for an ongoing supply of new driverless cars.

On the other hand, some pundits have predicted that we won't need as many cars as we have today, since a smaller number of ridesharing driverless cars will fulfill our driving needs, abetting the need for everyone to have a car.

No one knows.

Another facet to consider involves the pace at which high-tech might advance and thus cause a heightened turnover in self-driving cars.

Suppose the sensors and computer processors put into a driverless car are eclipsed in just a few years by faster, cheaper, and better sensors and computer processors.

If the sensors and processors of a self-driving car are built-in, meaning that you can't just readily swap them out, it could be that the another driving force for the quicker life cycle of a driverless car might be as a result of the desire to make use of the latest in high-tech.

The idea of retiring a driverless car in four years doesn't seem quite as shocking after analyzing the basis for such a belief.

Whether society is better off or not as a result of self-driving cars, and also the matter of those self-driving cars only lasting four years, it's a complex question and we'll need to see how this all plays out.

CHAPTER 8

ENTREPRENEURS

AND

AI SELF-DRIVING CARS

CHAPTER 8

ENTREPRENEURS
AND
AI SELF-DRIVING CARS

One of the most popular tropes in high-tech seems to be the notion that an enterprising entrepreneur could miraculously invent the next-gen earth-shattering doodad in their garage.

In fact, the start-up whiz might not even be using their own garage and instead might be toiling away in someone else's garage, such as one owned by a dear uncle or a neighbor that is okay with having a resident tinkerer that is aiming to change the world.

Time and again, we've all heard the stories about the Silicon Valley millionaires and zillionaires that began their arduous journey by using a soldering iron and a cheap keyboard to craft some breakthrough hardware and software for an ingenious system that ultimately took the marketplace by storm.

Here's a question worth considering: *Could a start-up entrepreneur invent a true self-driving car in their garage?*

The possibility stokes the imagination.

Perhaps right now there is an engineer or programmer in a nondescript garage that is on the verge of unveiling a true self-driving driverless car.

Can't wait to see it.

Meanwhile, let's unpack the matter.

Initial Wild Claims

Those of you that were paying attention to the initial impetus of self-driving cars might remember a few years ago when there were some wild claims by entrepreneurs boldly proclaiming that they could make a self-driving car.

The media loves to hear those kinds of outlandish claims and be the first to share a potential rags-to-riches tale.

What added to the confusion was the misunderstanding of what constitutes a true self-driving car.

Most would agree that a true self-driving or driverless car is one that drives entirely by itself, using AI technology. There is no requirement for a human driver to undertake the driving for a true self-driving car. The car is being driven by the automation, in an autonomous manner, removing the need for a human to perform the driving task.

We don't have such a self-driving driverless car as yet.

The roadway trials you hear about are based on a hoped-for driverless car that right now is only able to handle narrow circumstances of driving autonomously. Furthermore, by-and-large those roadway experiments include a back-up or safety driver, a human at the wheel, presumably ready (hopefully) to take over the driving if needed at a moment's notice.

There are also cars that are considered semi-autonomous that are entering into the marketplace. For a Level 2 and Level 3 car, these semi-autonomous cars require that a human driver be present and must be at the wheel of the vehicle. In that sense, the automation is co-sharing the driving task with the human. These kinds of cars have a type of technology referred to as ADAS (Advanced Driving Assistance Systems).

I am purposely bringing up the distinction between a truly autonomous car and a semi-autonomous car since it makes a big difference in the pursuit of self-driving tech.

In particular, the preponderance of initial claims by eager entrepreneurs was oftentimes mislabeled as an effort to develop a self-driving car, when instead it was primarily a quite narrow effort involving creating a semi-autonomous car (at best).

Unfortunately, the confounding aspect of intertwining true self-driving car possibilities with the piecemeal and less advanced ADAS tinkering led to marketplace bewilderment.

Why were the major automakers being upstaged by some nerdy developer that was working on a shoestring budget and yet apparently was able to eclipse the stuck-in-the-mud backward-looking car manufacturers?

The chagrin and frustration by the automakers could certainly be felt as they had to contend with explaining why their mega million-dollar budgets and hordes of design engineers were unable to do what an entrepreneur was doing in a garage.

Those start-up efforts ultimately failed or faltered, though a few did lead to some acqui-hires (a larger firm buys a company to acquire the talent) or eventually branched out and have continued their quest to this day, usually bankrolled by an automaker or a deep-pockets tech firm.

It Takes A Village

So far, I've covered the past and suggested that a garage-based entrepreneurial start-up to develop a true self-driving car was overall a bust.

What about now, would it be possible nowadays?

Unlikely.

Estimates indicate that today's modern cars have about 150 million lines of code in them, and for a self-driving car it could be somewhere near 250 million lines of code or more.

I assure you that even the most ingenious and fast-paced programmer is not going to create from-scratch the gargantuan 250 million lines of code, it's beyond any reasonable chance.

That being said, one can argue about the nature of lines of code.

It is well-known that you can potentially do the work of say ten lines of code in one line of code, depending upon what programming language you are using and how you are using it.

Furthermore, some argue that the number of lines of code being quoted for today's car automation is over-inflated since it includes the code underlying the operating system, the utilities, and other facets of the system that weren't necessarily written by the self-driving car developers (they instead have licensed or bought the other software to be underneath their software).

You could also point to the gradual emergence of open source software, which is gradually making its way into the self-driving car realm.

With open source, the software source code is made publicly available and anyone can incorporate it into their own system, though bound by certain restrictions and licensing aspects.

Thus, you might occasionally hear the story of a start-up whiz that with 2,000 lines of code has made an entire so-called self-driving car, which is usually based on the programmer piecing together the thousands or millions of lines of code from open source repositories and other avenues, and merely writing a small overarching piece that directs or coordinates the rest of the system.

Again, I'm declaring that this is not especially practical, and you shouldn't be misled by any such claims.

Generally, the rule-of-thumb is that it takes a village to create a self-driving car.

You need teams of experts in a wide range of realms that can come together and synergistically craft a self-driving car. There is a myriad of varying sensors on-board a self-driving car, including cameras, radar, LIDAR, ultra-sonic, and other specialized devices. There are computer processors needed, along with Machine Learning (ML) and Deep Learning (DL) models and capabilities. And so on.

The one-person effort is insufficient.

Consider too the kind of testing needed, encompassing closed track testing, simulation-based testing, and potentially public roadway testing. These are massive efforts. In addition, there is a lot of regulatory paperwork and approvals needed.

If we tried to fit the developers needed into a garage, the garage would have to be the size of a mighty large warehouse.

In any case, the point is that a true self-driving car is so complex, so large-scale, it is not going to be invented by an entrepreneur in a garage.

Lots Of Other Opportunities

For those wide-eyed entrepreneurs out there, I don't want my assertions herein to crush your dreams.

If you are desirous of doing a startup in the realm of self-driving cars, I want to encourage you to consider doing so. I say this because there are lots of outstanding opportunities in the assorted parts and pieces that go into a self-driving car.

You don't have to invent an entire self-driving car to become a Rockstar in the self-driving tech industry.

Set your sights on developing the next great Machine Learning algorithm that will vastly improve the ability to detect roadway objects.

Or, craft a new kind of Virtual World model that sits inside the AI system and provides a real-time indication of the traffic situation surrounding the self-driving car.

Maybe develop new hardware such as boosting the existing kinds of sensors on a driverless car, or perhaps invent an entirely new kind of sensor that nobody has yet identified.

The sky is the limit.

Here's some suggestions of areas that need further help:
- Sensor hardware and software
- Data storage and compression
- Sensor fusion
- Virtual world models
- AI system action plans
- Car controls activation
- Self-aware AI capabilities
- Machine Learning
- Deep Learning
- Car on-board networking

- V2V (Vehicle-to-Vehicle)
- In-car NLP (Natural Language Processing)
- Distributed AI
- Car cybersecurity
- Traffic simulations
- Car testing tools
- Etc.

Conclusion

Take a look in your garage, and if there's someone in there that is pining away at creating a true self-driving car, please gently let them know that it's going to be a tough road for them.

Probably best to consider tackling the myriad of unsolved problems that still challenge elements of the self-driving car field and see if a solution might be found. Getting your arms around pieces of the puzzle that fit into a true self-driving car provides ample opportunities.

Yes, glory, fame, wealth, and more beckons those of you working in your garages, since you might have the missing piece that completes the quest to develop a true self-driving car.

CHAPTER 9
AUTOPILOT CRASH LESSONS AND
AI SELF-DRIVING CARS

CHAPTER 9

AUTOPILOT CRASH LESSONS AND AI SELF-DRIVING CARS

The NTSB has released its official findings about a car crash that involved a Tesla Model S with its Autopilot-engaged that rammed into the back of a parked fire truck on a busy freeway in Southern California, occurring on a sunny morning of January 22, 2019.

NTSB investigators examined various collected evidence about the crash and interviewed the driver and an eyewitness, along with sorting through vehicle related data pertaining to the moments leading up to and at the moment of the incident.

In my initial overall review of the NTSB report, there are some important elements worthy of consideration as valuable lessons learned and I've detailed those points below.

Background About The Incident

As useful background about the incident, the Tesla was heading southbound on a busy freeway, the I-405, and came upon a fire truck that had responded to a prior incident involving a downed motorcyclist.

The fire truck had parked in the HOV lane to guard the area in front of the fire truck, allowing the fire department personnel and other first responders to aid in recovery of the motorcycle incident.

As is customary in such instances, the fire truck parked slightly askew, straddling the HOV lane, which meant that any upcoming traffic would presumably see that the fire truck was stationary and hopefully not be visually misled if the fire truck were instead placed at a straight ahead angle (i.e., an upcoming driver might not be sure if the fire truck was perhaps moving, maybe slowly forward, while by being askew, it is thought that the traffic will more readily realize the fire truck is parked).

The Tesla was in the HOV lane and coming up quickly toward the parked fire truck.

According to the driver of the Tesla, a somewhat large-sized vehicle such as a SUV was in front of the Tesla during the time leading up to the fire truck, and this other vehicle apparently blocked the view of being able to see the fire truck. At the last moment, the vehicle ahead of the Tesla opted to dart out of the HOV lane, and the Tesla proceeded to ram into the rear of the fire truck.

The Tesla driver survived the impact and was able to get out of the Tesla, stunned and yet able to walk where the incident scene was.

The Tesla had incurred a modest amount of damage including a crushed front bumper, buckled hood, broken headlights, shatter windshield, and other related collision damages.

The fire truck was struck at primarily the left rear area, which was the angled part of the fire truck closest to the straight-ahead impact by the Tesla.

A relatively minor amount of damage was done to the fire truck, and fortunately none of the nearby fire fighters were injured by the crash.

Let's now unpack salient aspects of the NTSB Report.

Driver Familiarity With Automation Being Used

One important aspect about the use of car automation involves whether the human driver knows how to use the automation.

Today's ADAS (Advanced Driver Assistance Systems) are becoming increasingly complex and there is concern that drivers might not properly employ the automation.

Consider these key aspects in this particular case.

Situation:

The driver of the Tesla had owned the car for about 6 months.

It was the first time that he had owned a Tesla, and previously had driven a Prius. He indicated that part of the reason he opted to purchase a Tesla was because of the Autopilot technology.

His daily commute to work consisted of taking the same path that he was undertaking on the day of the incident and he routinely used Autopilot during those trips.

Analysis:

This driver presumably knew enough about Autopilot to be familiar with it.

Had he just bought the car or if it was a rented car, he might have been in a posture of not knowing Autopilot and not known what its capabilities and limitations are. He routinely used Autopilot, and indeed his remarks during the interview with the NTSB reflected his general understanding about the Autopilot features.

Also, notably, he was driving in an area that he knew, rather than driving in say a new area that was unfamiliar to him.

Lessons:

The aspect that the driver was familiar with Autopilot provides both a positive and a negative in these kinds of situations.

Drivers can become lulled into thinking that the automation of the car will pretty much protect them and therefore they allow themselves to become complacent as a driver.

Over reliance on the automation is an easy trap to fall into. If you drive for many hours and hours, day after day, and the automation seems to be safely guiding your car, you can mistake that pattern to believe the automation is doing more than it really can.

Dovetail into the matter that the area being driven was familiar can provide a kind of double whammy, namely that the automation is in familiar territory and being used in a familiar way, all of which can cause a driver to let their guard down.

Sensors Aspects Are Crucial

The sensors built into the car and used for aiding the automation during the driving task are crucial to how the driving will be performed by the automated system.

An appropriate set of sensors, along with being varied so as to provide multiple perspectives are required, plus the sensor data needs to be assessed by the on-board sensor fusion capability to make a cohesive whole out of the piecemeal raw data detection being performed by the sensors.

Situation:

The driver of the Tesla indicated that when he bought the car, he had it fully inspected by a Tesla dealership, wanting to make sure that the used Tesla was in good shape. There were some repairs made and upon doing so he was apparently told that the Tesla Model S was ready for use.

Subsequently, according to the interview, he had the cameras on the front of the Tesla replaced, apparently twice, along with having either a radar or sonar unit also replaced.

On the day of the incident, he was operating on the Tesla Hardware Version 1 and had last received a firmware OTA (Over-The-Air) update on December 28, 2017, just about 25 days prior to the crash.

He also indicated that in his experience of using Autopilot, when the car was heading directly toward the sun, the Autopilot would at times not seem to be able to gauge sufficiently objects ahead of the car. He likened this to a person that might be squinting to see what's ahead when looking into the sun, and so he at times would turn-off the Autopilot and revert to purely manual control of the Tesla if the sunshine aspects seemed worrisome.

He indicated that the incident that morning did involve driving toward the sun.

Analysis:

We don't know why the cameras were apparently replaced, and nor why the sonar or radar was replaced. Whether this might be a factor related to the incident is seemingly unknown.

That being said, there hasn't been any stated indication in the NTSB Report that the Tesla itself was not functioning or that any of the sensors or automation systems were having any issues.

In terms of the Autopilot update, the aspect that it was recently undertaken implies that presumably the latest available version was on-board the vehicle, though the NTSB Report doesn't clarify whether or not a more recent version might have been available (and if so, whether it might have any relationship to the incident).

Lessons:

Drivers tend to over time discover facets about their cars, such as knowing that a car can handle left turns well but maybe gets sticky on right turns.

The same kind of driver discovery happens with the automation being used on a car, namely that the human driver gradually identifies quirks and nuances about the automation.

In this case, the driver said that he had discovered that sunlight shining directly at the front of the Tesla was able to at times create difficulties for the Autopilot.

There is a potential that the cameras might not be able to grab clear images or be otherwise somewhat confounded by a flood of sunshine, plus the captured images might not be readily interpreted by the Machine Learning system that is employed.

This also highlights the importance of having a multiple set of sensors and different types of sensors, such that if one particular sensor or a set of a particular kind of sensors are stymied, other sensors might make-up for the difficulty.

During sensor fusion, the data of the several sensors are pulled together in real-time and analyzed by the automation, trying to figure out the true nature of the driving scene, including whether to ignore sensory data that might be unreliable and opt to provide greater weight to other sensory data.

If perchance the cameras were hindered by the sunlight, what did the radar detect and how did the sensor fusion deliberate between the camera images interpretation and the radar data interpretation?

Did the angle of the parked fire truck potentially disturb the radar detection, maybe reducing the certainty of the radar return?

If there had been a LIDAR capability, a type of sensory device eschewed by Elon Musk and not included in Tesla's sensory suite, would it have aided in potentially detecting the fire truck within the final seconds remaining prior to impact?

LIDAR units are oftentimes placed on the top of a vehicle to gain a 360-degree perspective, and if so, would a sensory vantage point from the rooftop of the car had a heightened chance of detecting the parked fire truck sooner than the other sensory devices at lower points on the vehicle body?

Data About The Crash

You likely know that airplanes contain a so-called "black box" that collects vital data about a plane, doing so as a means to allow an after-crash analysis of what was occurring in the plane's systems at the time of the crash.

Referred to more formally as Event Data Recorders (EDR), we take it for granted that airplanes make use of them.

In the United States, the use of EDR's on cars is a voluntary activity by the car manufacturers and there is no federally mandated legal requirement that an EDR must be included into a normal car. Some automakers include an EDR, some do not.

There is an ongoing debate about whether or not an EDR should be a mandatory piece of equipment on cars.

Situation:

The Tesla did not have an Event Data Recorder, which as mentioned above is not a requirement.

In lieu of examining the data of an EDR post-crash, the NTSB sought out Tesla to provide data to the NTSB, which per the NTSB Report "Tesla wirelessly downloaded the recorder/Autopilot data from the crash involved vehicle post-crash; this data was provided to NTSB investigators."

The data indicated that the Tesla's ignition cycle had started about 66 minutes before the crash, meaning that the car had been turned-on for roughly 66 minutes prior to the crash.

Furthermore, the data showed that the Tesla was following a vehicle ahead of it, prior to the crash, and the system was adjusting the speed of the Tesla to maintain a relatively constant time-based distance to the "lead" vehicle.

According to the data, with approximately 4 to 7 seconds left to go before the crash occurred, the Tesla was "traveling at a consistent speed of about 21 mph, the lead vehicle was slowing." And, the "lead vehicle changed lanes at 3-4 seconds before the crash."

I'll come back to this data in a moment.

Analysis:

The data seems to match to the driver's remarks that he was following another vehicle while approaching the parked fire truck.

Plus, the data seems to support the indication by the Tesla driver that the vehicle ahead darted out of the lane just as the parked fire truck was a few seconds away.

Lessons:

The Tesla driver said that he didn't see the fire truck, presumably because his view was blocked by the vehicle ahead of him.

One of the potential aspects about using a fully rigged automated car that has a full suite of sensors is the possibility that it might be able to detect objects ahead that the human driver might not see. This capability obviously depends on the types of sensors used, along with where the sensors are placed onto the car.

This is not an easy matter, though, and it is possible that even the best of sensors might be blocked or obstructed.

In terms of the debate about having an EDR, some proponents argue that without an EDR, the post-crash investigation becomes overly dependent upon the car manufacturer and would presumably be reliant upon the car manufacturer to try and retrieve any data and provide the data in whole or in part to the investigators.

Detection And Reaction By The Automation

A human driver that becomes expectant of the car automation to take vital steps during a traffic exigency is assuming that the automation will appropriately detect a dire driving situation and then the automation will correspondingly take needed corrective action.

Situation:

Per the NTSB Report, once the vehicle ahead of the Tesla abruptly changed lanes, the data indicates that the "following distance of 33 meters at 4.1 seconds before the crash dramatically increased to 120 meters one second later; the 120 meter is a default value indicating that the system has not detected a vehicle in front."

Furthermore, "As the system no longer detected a lead vehicle 3-4 seconds before the crash, Autopilot started accelerating the Tesla toward the TACC-set cruise speed of 80 mph which the driver set nearly 5 minutes before the crash.

And, "At the time of the impact, the Tesla was traveling at the speed of 30.9 mph."

Finally, here's this essential and telling aspect too: "Data shows that about 490 msec before the crash, the system detected a stationary object in the path of the Tesla. At that time, the forward collision warning was activated; the system presented a visual and auditory warning."

The NTSB Report also states that the Automatic Emergency Braking (AEB) system did not engage and nor did the human driver engage the brakes at the time of the incident.

Analysis:

It would seem that once the lead vehicle got out of the lane, presumably at that juncture there might have been a chance to detect the parked fire truck, assuming that it wasn't somehow feasible to have earlier detected it.

Perhaps there were three to four seconds or less that might have been available, according to the reported data, though it is difficult to say. It appears to be the case that with about a half-second left to go, the system did presumably detect the fire truck.

It is problematic to try and play with those few seconds in-absence of knowing more about how the automation is structured and designed, since there is time needed for the sensors to collect data, there is time needed for the sensor fusion to assess the data, there is time needed for the computer processors to figure out what it means and what to do next, etc.

Interestingly, the forward collision warning was apparently issued to alert the driver (with a half-second left to go), though the AEB wasn't activated.

Lessons:

Automation for cars can be a complex intertwining set of somewhat disparate components, each of which has their own particular functionality, and yet overall those components in-the-end need to work as a tightly organized cohesive whole.

The timing of how those components work can be crucial to the driving task.

The Driver

For the automakers that are producing Level 2 and Level 3 cars, they are apt to indicate that the ultimate responsibility for the driving of the car is the human driver.

Thus, essentially no matter what the automation does or does not do, the argument made is that it was on the shoulders of the human driver and whatever happens in a car accident rests with the driver, not with the automation.

Situation:

The Tesla driver indicated that he had his left hand on his knee and that his fingers were lightly touching the steering wheel, and his right hand was free, though he also indicated that he might have had a coffee cup in his right hand.

He indicated that he was not using his cell phone at the time of the crash.

An eyewitness in a car that was nearby the Tesla claimed that the Tesla driver was looking downward, as though looking at some device in their hand, and the eyewitness said that the Tesla driver did not look-up at all to see the fire truck.

Analysis:

Was the Tesla driver paying attention and got caught unawares by the sudden lane change of the car ahead?

Or, was the Tesla driver not paying attention, perhaps believing that the automation was doing just fine, and distracted by something else inside the car, such as the coffee or a cell phone?

Lessons:

There is a growing concern that drivers in Level 2 and Level 3 cars might readily allow themselves to become distracted from the driving task, and as such, some automakers are adding more and more tech to try and ascertain whether a driver is remaining alert to the driving effort.

Conclusion

For those that are concerned about the name Autopilot, which has stirred controversy as a naming of automation that for which could be construed as misleadingly suggesting the automation is able to perform in a true fully autonomous manner, the Tesla driver remarked during his interview that he felt that the name was not accurate since the vehicle does not fully drive itself.

In addition, there are some that are concerned that drivers that are first stepping behind the steering wheel of these partially automated cars will not properly understand what the car does and what they need to do as a driver.

Oftentimes, the automaker will assert that the owner's manual lays out the operations of the vehicle and therefore the first-time driver of such a car is informed as such via the owner's manual.

The Tesla driver said that he had an owner's manual but had never looked at it, and instead when he bought the Tesla he had a salesman take a few minutes to show him how to operate the Tesla. Whether having a salesman quickly show someone the full depth of features and limitations of a Level 2 or Level 3 car is sufficient for proper operation of the car is open to debate.

Overall, for each of these instances of a car crash involving a Level 2 or Level 3 car, it is important and useful to consider lessons that can be gleaned, hopefully providing insightful guidance to the further refinement of ADAS and also for the pursuit of true self-driving cars.

CHAPTER 10

U.N. FRAMEWORK

AND

AI SELF-DRIVING CARS

CHAPTER 10

U.N. FRAMEWORK

AND

AI SELF-DRIVING CARS

Trying to drive a car in a foreign land can be daunting.

The car itself is usually pretty much the same in terms of its operational characteristics, meaning that there is a steering wheel, a brake pedal, and accelerator pedal, and other driving related controls that you can readily figure out.

Where the tough part comes to play involves the act of driving the car and dealing with the differences when performing the driving task.

There are likely different kinds of roadway signage than you might have seen in your home country. Fortunately, those signs are usually relatively standardized and visually easy to understand, even if you aren't especially familiar with the signage being used.

Another difficulty can be dealing with the laws and regulations governing driving in the country that you are cruising around in.

Yes, by-and-large the nature of those rules is somewhat the same from country to county, though there are enough subtle differences that you could find yourself getting a traffic ticket for reasons that might at first seem surprising.

A somewhat hidden or less realized difference involves the culture of the driving practices in the country that you are enjoying time behind the wheel.

I say enjoying but the word might instead be enduring since the cultural norms of driving could be radically different than what you are normally accustomed to seeing. In some places, driving a car is considered an absolute free-for-all. Drivers weave into spots that you didn't think a car could go. The driving distances between cars becomes an inch away nightmare of seemingly continual battles over which car will get the right-of-way.

Essentially, one might suggest that the hardware of car driving is about the same, while the "software" of driving is oftentimes significantly different.

In the case of human drivers, the "software" refers to the mental models underlying the driving task.

You need to adjust your mental viewpoint of how to drive a car and try to fit within the approaches and methods considered acceptable in the foreign land. For most seasoned drivers, you can usually get up-to-speed relatively quickly, though the new approach can be a sweat inducing seat-of-the-pants indoctrination to a different mindset or mode of driving a car.

Here's an intriguing and important question: How will the AI systems of self-driving cars cope with driving in different countries?

It's actually a lot more complicated and eyebrow raising then you might assume.

Let's unpack the matter.

United Nations Framework Released

Part of the reason that I bring up this topic is that the United Nations has just released a new framework aiming to help globalize self-driving cars.

Various experts from around the globe are working on the *World Forum For Harmonization Of Vehicle Regulations*, including representatives from the United States, Japan, European Union (EU), China, and other countries. The World Forum has a subgroup that was formed last year to focus particularly on autonomous related vehicles, a formal body known as the *Working Party On Automated/Autonomous And Connected Vehicles* (GRVA).

To clarify, there are true self-driving cars, which most would agree are considered at a Level 4 and Level 5 of the driving autonomy scale and involve the AI driving the car entirely and without a human driver present, and then there are semi-autonomous cars which require that a human driver co-share the driving task.

The co-shared driving or semi-autonomous cars are labeled as Level 2 and Level 3, of which the Level 3 cars are just starting to enter into the marketplace. Gradually, advanced automation is increasingly participating in the driving task with human drivers, something referred to as ADAS (Advanced Driving Assistance Systems), which bodes well in some respects and yet also has raises some alarming concerns (see my piece here covering those concerns).

There aren't any true self-driving cars as yet, though experimental roadway trials are taking place with autonomous cars that will presumably someday be readily available for use.

There is ongoing controversy underlying the idea that we are perhaps all participating in a guinea pig manner by letting these Level 4 and potentially Level 5 driverless cars be on our public roadways prior to them being fully tested and vetted for safety.

Returning to the matter of globalization, the advanced automation or the AI that's supposed to drive a car is vulnerable to the same kinds of county-to-country difficulties that a human driver might experience.

Suppose an AI system is developed to drive in the United States.

Overall, the AI is directly programmed to abide by our rules and cultural practices, plus it will likely pick-up many of those customs during its Machine Learning (ML) and Deep Learning (DL) efforts. The ML and DL usually examines tons of driving data to ferret out patterns of driving and then tries to adhere to the patterns identified.

In a sense, you could suggest that the AI in this use case is becoming a U.S.-based driver, which means that if you then take that same self-driving car to another country, the AI would be as baffled and confused as taking a driver from the United States and plucking them behind the wheel in that foreign land.

What's though much worse is that the AI is not at all like a human in that the AI lacks common-sense reasoning and otherwise cannot likely adjust on-the-fly in the same way that a human driver could.

The AI self-driving car would be a duck out of water.

Other nearby human drivers would have to avoid it or might even take advantage of its wooden and out-of-place driving practices. All in all, the new setting could sadly produce car accidents and even be unsafe for pedestrians and others that are using those roadways.

One hope is that perhaps a globalization roadmap might aid in ensuring that these self-driving cars can accommodate being used in various and multiple countries.

Facets Of The U.N. Framework

Here's the main areas of attention in the U.N. framework:
a. System Safety
b. Failsafe Response
c. Human Machine Interface
d. Object Event Detection and Response (OEDR)
e. Conditions under which the automated system will operate
f. Validation for System Safety
g. Cybersecurity
h. Software Updates
i. Data storage and Event data recorder (EDR)

Keep in mind that this is the initial release of the framework and primarily sets the stage for what will be happening next.

Thus, if you are hoping to see a detailed indication of the self-driving car globalization particulars, you'll need to wait. Draft proposals offering such details are expected to be released in the next several months.

Right now, the framework is an articulation of the overarching working principles.

For some, this is a bit of a disappointment for those awaiting the fuller depictions, but it seems reasonable to have the working principles posted now and allow us all a moment to reflect on the core vision.

One other qualm some have about the release is that it does not yet encompass some additional areas that many are waiting to see covered, including these (I've listed the additional areas starting with the letter "j" since they are ultimately going to be presumably prioritized into the ongoing foregoing list):
j. Vehicle maintenance and inspection
k. Consumer Education and Training
l. Crashworthiness and Compatibility
m. Post-crash AV behavior

Controversy About Safety Definition

Critics are already carping about the manner in which safety is being defined.

Here's how the safety vision is stated:

"The level of safety to be ensured by automated/autonomous vehicles implies that "an automated/autonomous vehicle shall not cause any non-tolerable risk", meaning that automated/autonomous vehicle systems, under their automated mode ([ODD/OD]), shall not cause any traffic accidents resulting in injury or death that are reasonably foreseeable and preventable."

It is somewhat of a mouthful, so let's parse the statement and see where the controversy lies.

Focus on the last part of the sentence that says the automation or AI should not "cause" any traffic accidents that "result in injury or death" and for which those caused traffic accidents were "reasonably foreseeable and preventable."

About The Cause

I'll start by picking on the word "cause."

The easy example of causing a car accident would be if the AI opted to veer into another car and outright rammed into it. If a human driver did the same thing, we'd all pretty much agree that they (the driver) caused the accident.

Suppose though that you were driving your car and changed lanes, and in so doing the car in the lane that you came into happened to tap on their brakes, meanwhile the car behind them rammed into that car because the other driver was caught by surprise at the braking action.

Who "caused" the car accident?

We have an elaborate process of insurance companies, police reports, forensic accident experts, and other ways in which we ultimately assess the cause of car accidents.

This is worth mentioning because an AI self-driving car could potentially take actions that could contribute toward a car accident, yet you might claim that it did not cause the car accident per se.

Do we want to have AI self-driving cars that might be somehow legally driving in a means that isn't the direct cause of car accidents and yet it's driving practices could be said to be fostering car accidents?

About The Injury Or Death Provision

Another qualm about the safety definition involves the phrase "result in injury or death."

You are driving your car in a parking lot and hit another car that is backing out of a parking space. You aren't hurt, and nor are the passengers in the other car.

Some are suggesting that the safety definition is letting the automation or AI off-the-hook for causing any kind of car accident that doesn't involve injury or death yet might nonetheless have property damages.

Do we want to have AI self-driving cars that can get away with a "no harm, no foul" driving practice that includes ramming into buildings, cars, and other items of property, as long as a human wasn't injured or killed?

About The Foreseeable And Preventable

The final words in the safety definition refer to aspects that are reasonably foreseeable and preventable.

You are driving down the street and a ball suddenly bounces onto the roadway from an adjacent grassy park. We've all been conditioned by our driving training and driving experiences to realize that where a bouncing ball goes there might soon be a running child.

A human driver would likely slow down and be watching for that child that might soon dart after the bouncing ball.

An advanced driving system or AI might not be programmed and nor have had ML/DL that gives it an anticipatory capability to predict that the ball presages a running child.

My point is that we can argue quite a bit about what constitutes a reasonable kind of sensibility about being able to foresee and then prevent driving incident. The example about the ball and the child is perhaps an obvious one.

Daily, we face zillions of driving situations for which you could debate whether a car accident could have been "reasonably" foreseen, let alone whether it could have been "reasonably" prevented.

For AI self-driving cars, one of the thorniest and yet to be ascertained criteria involves what we would all concur is a "reasonableness" in terms of being able to anticipate and prevent the self-driving car from getting into a car accident.

Conclusion

Globalization of AI self-driving cars is something that many are not yet focusing on due to the aspect that they say we need to walk before we can crawl.

In other words, it is easier to concentrate your resources on making an AI self-driving car that can work properly in one country, while it is said to be overwhelming and distracting to try simultaneously to figure out how to contend with driving aspects in other countries.

Yes, a heads-down approach to make self-driving cars safe for operating in solely one country is perhaps prudent to prevent trying to chew on more than you can eat, yet at the same time there does need to be someone looking beyond the single country perspective and taking a global view.

I'll be updating you from time-to-time with the progress of the U.N. efforts and meanwhile keep your eyes out for any foreign AI self-driving cars that are out-of-place and trying to drive on your roadways but lacks an international globalized capability.

CHAPTER 11

SPORTS CARS

AND

AI SELF-DRIVING CARS

CHAPTER 11

SPORTS CARS

AND

AI SELF-DRIVING CARS

Some say that being at the steering wheel of a top-end sports car is like being in driving heaven.

You feel the surge of bone-rattling raw automotive power at your command, and skillfully take tight turns that would make most people blanch with fear. With gentle touches on the accelerator pedal and a quick yank of the gear shift knob, you find yourself zipping along on the open road and become totally immersed in a sense of blissful thrill and utter freedom.

Suppose though that the sports car was being driven by an AI-system, one that could drive the so-called "hypercar" as good as a human can (a hypercar is automotive insider lingo for the fastest and oftentimes most expensive top-end cars).

Indeed, imagine that the AI could even exceed the capabilities of a normal human driver and push the sports car to limits that a sports car pro would likely blanch at.

Would you still want to be riding in the top-end sports car?

Or, would the inability to drive the vehicle by yourself, using your own hands and feet, be such a disappointment that you would say ixnay to riding around in one?

Though some say that self-driving tech and sports cars are a kind of oxymoron, suggesting that never the two shall meet, there's more to the story than meets the eye.

Let's unpack the matter.

Consider Porsches And Self-Driving

One of the most notable ongoing debates about whether top-end sports cars will ultimately be infused with AI true self-driving car capabilities seems to surround Porsches.

In 2016, a long time ago in the unrelenting quest toward more advanced driving features for cars, the Porsche CEO Oliver Blume was quoted as saying that "One wants to drive a Porsche by oneself."

At the time, many pundits interpreted this noteworthy and somewhat satisfying remark to mean that there would never be a self-driving version of a Porsche.

Case closed.

Then, just last year in 2018, the Porsche North American CEO Klaus Zellmer said this: "Our plan is to always have the steering wheel and always have the pedals and potentially to even have the manual gearbox to really engage with the car and to do it all yourself."

This crucial comment would tend to reaffirm the human driver as the only true driver of a sports car, though Zellmer also indicated this: "But, our customers always want it all. They want the possibility to use autonomous drive mode, but they want to really engage with the car as well."

The advent of the new Porsche Taycan, an Electrical Vehicle (EV) sports car, sparks anew the debate about whether sports cars are going to be self-driving or not.

Since most self-driving cars are tending toward EV's, and now that Porsche is bringing forth an EV sports car, perhaps the day of driverless sports cars is dawning upon us.

For those that have long been on the side of "you'll pry the steering wheel from my cold dead hands" camp, it is important to realize that there has been a broadening definition associated with self-driving and sports cars, one that maybe you like or hate, depending upon your viewpoint.

Sharply put, the question is not whether sports cars will have self-driving, but instead whether they will have only self-driving and exclude human driving as a possibility.

This is a significant point worthy of elaboration.

Self-Driving Mode

Let's take a moment and sort out the various ways in which self-driving tech applies to cars.

There are semi-autonomous cars that require a human driver to be present and able to drive the car, doing so in a co-sharing arrangement with the automation of the car. These are often referred to as Level 2 and Level 3 cars and make use of ADAS (Advanced Driver-Assistance Systems).

Even more cutting-edge are the truly autonomous cars, ones that are self-driving and there is no human involved in the driving task. These driverless cars are considered at the Level 4 and Level 5 of self-driving autonomy (none fully exist as yet, and the roadway trials taking place are at best the lower end of a Level 4).

For a sports car, you could be the type of person that insists there not be any ADAS or only very limited ADAS, since you don't want the automation to be in your way and be undermining your desired control and command over the vehicle.

I doubt that those types of drivers are going to prevail and inexorably the vaunted sports car will increasingly have ADAS.

It could be that the ADAS allows for having a lighter or heavier hand in co-sharing the driving task with the human driver, perhaps a knob that allows you to select high or low for the automated assistance, but nonetheless the ADAS is going to be there and you aren't likely to see sports cars without it.

The real crux of the debate centers around true self-driving capabilities.

Some see this self-driving topic as an all-or-nothing proposition, namely a sports car either has self-driving and it is always and only being driven by the AI, or it does not have self-driving and thus it is a semi-autonomous car that involves a human and AI co-sharing the driving task.

Must it be that way?

A counter-argument is that you could have true self-driving, which would mean that the AI is driving and there is no human driving involved, and yet also have a human-driving mode that allows a human driver to disengage the self-driving and revert the car back to being semi-autonomous.

For example, you drive your sports car on the scenic coastal highway and reach your destination in Malibu, aiming to dine at a fine restaurant overlooking the sea. There doesn't appear to be a valet standing at the entrance of the eatery, so you get out of your car and turn-on the self-driving feature, telling the car to find a suitable parking spot. Away goes your sports car, driving itself until it manages to neatly park the car for you.

As suggested by the insight that customers will want what they want, I think you'd be hard-pressed to have even the most fanatical sports car fan be upset that the self-driving mode was used to park the car.

In fact, it is likely the sports car driver would insist upon and be overtly perturbed if they didn't have that kind of self-driving capability, especially if other driverless cars were on the market and could do likewise (and were cheaper cars!).

Overall, it could be that a car, including sports cars, might have a true self-driving mode and yet also still retain the semi-autonomous mode, allowing for a choice between which mode you might opt to use.

There are admittedly some thorny legal issues to be dealt with in such an arrangement, including that existing laws tend to require that if there are driving controls then those driving controls must act in a prescribed manner and the car can't just opt to ignore those driving controls when a human attempts to use them.

If such laws could be adjusted, the car could either be in the self-driving mode, or it would be in the semi-autonomous mode, and never would it be in both modes at once. The self-driving mode is mutually exclusive of the semi-autonomous mode.

This does though bring up a bit of a conundrum.

We'd better consider the downsides of such an arrangement.

Self-Driving As All Or Nothing

First, just to clarify, in the scenario being postulated, it is assumed that once the self-driving mode is engaged there is no human driving involved.

One question that immediately arises about the self-driving car mode aspect involves when the human can choose to take over the driving and opt to disengage the driverless function.

If a human driver can disengage the driverless function at any time, it would imply that while the car is going 70 miles per hour on the freeway and the human suddenly decides to take over the wheel, the self-driving feature "gives up" the car controls to the human.

This might be a bad idea.

The human driver could be drunk and has stupidly and wrongly decided to disengage the driverless feature.

Or, maybe the driver inadvertently touched the disengage button, and terrifyingly realizes that they are now supposed to be driving the car.

As such, those that are proponents of the self-driving car "mode" say that there would need to be stated conditions under which you could disengage the driverless feature. It could be that there isn't any means to disengage the self-driving if the car is underway, and instead, you need to come to a complete stop and then can turn-off the driverless mode and take over the controls.

Having a driverless mode that can be switched on or off, even if done in some prescribed and thoughtful manner, doesn't appeal to those that argue the self-driving has to be all-or-nothing, meaning that a car is either a self-driving car or it is not a self-driving car.

For those that believe the self-driving car will be a means to reduce or possibly eliminate car crashes, they would find abhorrent the notion that a self-driving car could sometimes be self-driving and at other times be human-driven.

The moment you open the door to any amount of human driving, it means that you are once again likewise opening the door toward human drivers that will cause car-related injuries and deaths. Remove the human driver from the equation and ensure that only AI driving is allowed, and thus presumably no more worries about those pesky and unreliable human drivers.

Though the aim to ultimately get rid of all human driving might be laudable, no one can say whether we all will agree to such a condition.

Will people really be willing to give up their "right" to drive (well, it's a privilege, granted by the government, but in any case, people tend to think of it as an inalienable right)?

There are approximately 250 million conventional cars in the United States alone, and once self-driving cars arrive (the kind that are only self-driving), those will be doing so among a lot of ongoing human-driven driving. For the foreseeable future, true self-driving cars that are exclusively and only self-driving are going to be mixing with human-driven cars.

That being the case, some would say that having self-driving cars that provide a self-driving mode and yet also still allow human driving would not be out-of-place with the mix of cars that will be on our roadways anyway.

Furthermore, for Level 4 cars, self-driving is limited to stipulated ODD's (Operational Design Domains), consisting of the car manufacturer specifying under which conditions the self-driving will properly operate.

An automaker might state that their self-driving car works only in sunny weather, and the self-driving capability won't engage when there is rain or snow or will disengage once rain or snow starts to appear.

Presumably, the Level 4 cars will still have human driving controls, allowing for a human driver to drive a car that has reached the limit of its ODD.

Just because there is rain, you aren't likely to be willing to have your self-driving car sitting around and waiting for sunshine to appear. Instead, you are bound to decide that you'll go ahead and drive the car, and once the weather changes then perhaps reengage the self-driving capability again (some pundits insist that Level 4 cars should only be driven by the automation, thus, once the car has exceeded its ODD, it will become a multi-ton paperweight).

Overall, considering that Level 4 cars might continue to have driving controls, the debate about having a self-driving mode is not quite so farfetched.

The use case that makes the matter more vexing involves the Level 5 cars, which don't yet exist, and we don't really know when they will be achieved (some say not for a very long time).

Utopian World Of Only Self-Driving Cars

The grand vision is that we will someday have only Level 5 self-driving cars on our roadways.

In this Utopian viewpoint, there won't be any human driving at all.

Self-driving cars will presumably eliminate car crashes (not quite true, as I've debunked), and the AI systems will communicate with each other via V2V (vehicle-to-vehicle) electronic communications, allowing for the smoothing out of traffic snarls and other adverse roadway circumstances.

I would guess that it will take numerous generations of us humans to gradually believe that the legal removal of human driving is something we all agree is worthwhile and willingly accept.

You could then assert that arguing about self-driving cars that are exclusively self-driving is somewhat premature, or I suppose the other side of the coin would be that it is a holistic look down-the-road at a faraway future we might envision.

Another option involves considering having self-driving cars that are on our roadways in special lanes or otherwise set apart from the rest of conventional traffic.

Thus, no need to wait for a world where all conventional cars are gone.

This could be done, though the economic cost and infrastructure efforts would be relatively significant, raising questions about whether doing so would be worthwhile.

Riding In Self-Driving Sports Cars

Earlier, the question had been posed about whether people would be interested in riding inside a sports car and yet not be driving the sports car, instead allowing the AI to self-drive the top-end vehicle.

There would be situations that a sports car driver might prefer to have the self-driving be undertaken, such as the example of parking the car.

Perhaps an astute driver that realized they were too tired or maybe too tipsy would sensibly engage the self-driving mode.

Maybe the sports car driver would want to observe how the AI drove the car, learning some nifty tricks and techniques for when they as a human opt to drive the high-performance vehicle.

And so on.

You can certainly anticipate that people that aren't comfortable driving a sports car at all would undoubtedly relish being able to go for a ride in a sports car that was self-driving, especially if the driverless mode was as good as or maybe even better than a human driver.

Imagine the excitement of feeling what the sports car can do, such as the Taycan that reportedly can go from 0 to 60 in about 2.6 to 3 seconds, all being driven by the AI system (if ever so outfitted).

Of course, one question arises concerning where could you experience the full depth of the sports car performance?

You aren't going to get much of a thrill presumably on freeways that limit your speed to 70 miles per hour.

Sure, you can have the driverless feature take those corners with the tires peeling and can possibly get the AI to do some modest sporty driving, but other than if you go for a ride on a closed track, you probably won't get the full sport performance experience.

In theory, the AI system would be purposely crafted to allow only legal driving, meaning that there's not going to be any high-speed excursions that take the car to its top speeds and go beyond the traffic laws of your locale.

Conclusion

One final thought involves sports car ownership.

There are some that seem to try and intertwine the self-driving car aspects of a sports car with the ownership aspects of a sports car.

In other words, the argument goes that if sports cars are self-driving, those driverless cars won't be owned by individuals, and instead will be owned by corporations that have those self-driving cars in fleets.

I don't ascribe to that theory.

My somewhat contrarian view is that we are going to have individual ownership of self-driving cars, including sports cars.

I argue that the money to be made by ridesharing your self-driving car will create a large cottage industry of people aiming to make some bucks from their driverless cars. While you are at work or asleep, your self-driving car will be roaming the streets and making money for you.

Therefore, I vehemently disagree with the assertion that if sports cars do get outfitted with self-driving tech that it means the death knell for sports car ownership by individuals.

It likely would likely promote individual ownership, potentially making the high-end expensive sports cars financially available to those that heretofore could not afford one.

That does raise a whole another topic, namely whether sports cars will lose their prestige and panache if it turns out they can be driven by AI and undermines the belief by some that driving a sports car is a uniquely human attribute.

I'm sure that there are those in the high-end sports enclave that would be dismayed to think that just anyone might soon be able to go for a ride in a fancy sports car, and if so, how such a change might impact societal perceptions of sports cars.

For the moment, those of you that love your sports cars, make hay while you can, though safely so.

CHAPTER 12

RAILROAD CROSSINGS

AND

AI SELF-DRIVING CARS

CHAPTER 12

RAILROAD CROSSINGS

AND

AI SELF-DRIVING CARS

Stop, look, and listen.

That's the customary sage advice for car drivers that come upon a railroad crossing.

Do you abide by that simple rules-of-the-road driving principle?

Many drivers do not.

In fact, you probably don't put much thought these days toward railroad crossings at all and are apt to do nothing more than a cursory glance before you zip across those bothersome railroad tracks that seem to mar the roadway ahead of you.

Well, don't be quite so quick to treat railroad crossings with such little respect.

According to compiled statistics, every 90 minutes in the United States a vehicle and a train collide.

That's a staggering and somber stat.

Train-vehicle crashes are a lot more common than most people assume they are.

Plus, sadly, injuries and deaths are the likely result of cars and trains opting to ram into each other. There are about 500 deaths each year in the United States due to failures to safety navigate a railroad crossing, amounting to about 20,000 deaths over the last forty years.

We are nearing the annual U.S. Rail Safety Week, taking place during the week of September 22 to September 28, and it might be worthwhile to remind your loved ones about the dangers of driving thoughtlessly at railroad crossings.

Indeed, you might watch your social media trends for the #STOPTrackTragedies to see some heart wrenching stories about what can happen in train-vehicle encounters.

Here's perhaps another surprise for you, namely that railroad crossings are much more prevalent than you might believe.

In the United States, there are approximately 128,000 public railroad crossings. Throughout the U.S. there are over 180,000 miles of railroad track.

Overall, railroads are still a significant part of the transportation fabric of our country.

I realize that some of you might be eager to point out that all a driver needs to do is obey a railroad crossing gate. If the gate is down, don't go around it, and just wait for the train to pass. That seems to take care of having to be concerned about railroad crossings.

Case closed.

Not so.

Sorry to say that only about one-third of all railroad crossings have a gate.

That means that two-thirds of railroad crossings do not have a gate. Numerically, two-thirds of the total number of railroad crossings comes out to about 84,500 crossings that do not have any gate.

Some people seem to think that if there isn't a gate, it implies the railroad crossing isn't dangerous. The logic seems to be that certainly the railroad bosses would put up a gate where it is needed, and therefore not put up gates where they are not needed.

That's not compelling logic.

When you come upon a railroad crossing that lacks a gate, it is on your shoulders as a driver to proceed safely.

I know that you might tend to assume that a train will certainly stop in time if your car perchance ends-up on the tracks, but a train moving at 55 miles per hour takes a mile or more to come to a stop.

Don't expect a locomotive conductor to save your hide, it's a lousy bet.

Since human drivers seem to be lacking in vigilance when crossing over railroad tracks, maybe we can solve the problem via the advent of self-driving cars.

This brings up an interesting question: Will AI-driven self-driving cars be safer than human drivers when it comes to dealing with railroad crossings?

The answer is maybe, rather than an outright and unequivocal yes, which I realize seems astonishing, so let's unpack the matter.

Self-Driving Cars And Railroad Crossings

I'll be focusing on true self-driving cars, rather than cars that perchance have advanced automation but still require a human driver at the wheel.

True self-driving cars are ones that have the AI exclusively doing the driving. Usually referred to as Level 4 and Level 5, there isn't a human driver involved in the driving act.

In contrast, a Level 2 and Level 3 are considered semi-autonomous cars, requiring a human driver to co-share the driving task. This co-sharing arrangement unfortunately has some inherent problems and concerns, and drivers need to be wary of allowing over-reliance on their ADAS (Advanced Driver-Assistance Systems).

Some pundits seem to assume that an AI system will be all-knowing and therefore magically be able to cope with any kind of driving situation.

That's just not the case.

Consider the nature of dealing with railroad crossings.

Yes, you could program an AI system to undertake certain prescribed steps when encountering a railroad crossing, and it likely would unfailingly try to carry out those steps. In that sense, you might argue that the AI would be more reliable than a human driver, since humans are bound to be inconsistent in their driving practices or might be drunk or simply inattentive.

The first hurdle though that the AI has to overcome is detecting that a railroad crossing even exists.

For humans, we are apt to see a sign that says railroad crossing ahead, along with noticing markings on the roadway that also forewarn about the crossing. We can usually see the railroad tracks implanted into the roadway surface. We might also be able to see down the railroad tracks and observe that they stretch some distance down to the left or right of where the tracks cross the road.

These are all vital clues that a railroad crossing exists, and we ought to be driving cautiously, accordingly.

Getting an AI system to readily figure out that a railroad crossing exists is harder than how humans do so.

The cameras of the self-driving car need to stream images of the driving scene and then scour the digitized video to find any railroad warning signs and railroad tracks that are on the roadway ahead.

Regrettably, the radar sensors and the LIDAR sensors are not especially helpful during this detection effort since they are less likely to pick-up the subtleties of the railroad crossing telltale aspects. That's a shame because self-driving cars are best suited to holistically ascertain their surroundings, making use of sensor fusion to bring together multiple forms of sensory input into a synergistic whole.

Whenever a self-driving car is reliant on only one kind of sensor, it can be a myopic way of fully gleaning what is going on.

Suppose too that the cameras are somewhat obscured by bad weather and cannot get sharp and clean images of the roadway ahead. Perhaps too the railroad markings and signs are in a dilapidated state, having been worn down over the years or marred with graffiti.

All in all, the point being that it is not assured with 100% certainty that a self-driving car will always detect that a railroad crossing is coming up ahead.

Humans can certainly also fail to detect railroad crossings, so don't misunderstand that maybe I'm suggesting that humans are infallible. Instead, the crux of the matter is that an AI system won't necessarily be perfect at identifying a railroad crossing either.

We could though speculate that at least we could program the AI to not do stupid things like try to go around a railroad gate that is blocking cars from proceeding across the railroad tracks.

As such, one would certainly hope that the number of train-vehicle crashes would lessen by merely ensuring that the AI abides by the rules-of-the-road, which we know humans are prone to not strictly observe.

Self-Driving Tech Added Advantages

One notable capability that would help the AI do a reasonably good job at detecting the existence of a railroad crossing would be the use of advanced GPS and hyper mapping systems.

Presumably, self-driving cars are going to have topnotch GPS capabilities and be armed with the latest and greatest high-def maps. In that case, the self-driving car could consult the map and GPS, and hopefully the railroad crossing is already electronically marked on the map.

The AI system could then reaffirm that a railroad crossing exists up ahead, having been forewarned by referring to the GPS and the electronic on-board maps, and then use its own sensors to verify that the railroad crossing is there.

Furthermore, we'll eventually have V2I (vehicle-to-infrastructure) electronic communications that will entail having our roadway infrastructure send out electronic signals to alert self-driving cars about roadway artifacts and conditions. If a bridge is out, the bridge itself might be emitting via an Internet of Things (IoT) device that any cars approaching the bridge should pursue a different path.

Railroad crossings that today are outfitted with flashing lights and gate arms could be augmented by having V2I devices to broadcast the existence of the railroad crossing and provide the status of any nearby trains.

Another detection factor that human drivers often use is the fact that the traffic around them is likely also coming to a halt due to a railroad crossing.

Thus, even if you fail to realize that a railroad crossing exists, you can see other cars around you that "mysteriously" are coming to a stop, and you might logically deduce that something is afoot, perhaps then noticing a huge angry train that's barreling down the tracks toward the crossing.

Likewise, AI that is properly programmed would notice the traffic surrounding the self-driving car and possibly piece together that if other cars are stopping, it might suggest that the self-driving car needs to also come to a stop.

Yet another upcoming feature of self-driving cars and connectedness consists of V2V (vehicle-to-vehicle) electronic communication.

This will be a means of having the AI system of a self-driving car communicate with the AI system of other nearby self-driving cars.

Potentially, a self-driving car that has come upon a railroad crossing could send out a message to other self-driving cars approaching the same spot and alert those AI systems that a train is coming along.

In theory, the trains themselves might also be able to do V2V, meaning that a rushing train would be broadcasting to nearby vehicles that the train is coming to town and watch out. Any V2V equipped car, truck, van, or other kind of vehicle would get an electronic notification from the train itself.

Edge Cases Are Tough

On the surface, it appears that the AI driving system has all the advantages for properly coping with railroad crossings.

If so, why are there any qualms or potential dangers for self-driving cars that come upon a railroad crossing?

Time to consider the myriad of edges cases that can arise.

An edge case or sometimes referred to as a corner case involves aspects that might be beyond the core elements of a given task, allowing you to set them aside for the moment, temporarily, but that ultimately could occur and therefore might be devastating since they weren't fully considered upfront.

Here's one: Imagine that a self-driving car safely proceeded to cross a set of railroad tracks, and then got stuck amid the railroad tracks.

If this seems farfetched, I'd say that it could happen, though admittedly rare, yet there's always the chance that any car could suffer a mechanical problem and suddenly breakdown or otherwise falter once it got onto the tracks.

Let's agree it is an edge case.

What happens now that the self-driving car is stuck on the tracks?

Well, the AI system might not be able to figure out that it is stuck.

Or, it might determine that it cannot move, but has no provision in the system action efforts of what to do next.

As an edge case, the AI developers might have left this seemingly obscure use case to someday be dealt with, and unfortunately the fielded AI doesn't have any contingencies ready for the circumstance.

For a human passenger inside the self-driving car, they might be perplexed about why the self-driving car has come to a halt. The AI Natural Language Processing (NLP), akin to a Siri or Alexa conversational capability, might be insufficiently programmed and unable to explain what has taken place.

We don't even know that the AI could now ascertain whether a train might be coming. If the self-driving car is facing forward, and the train is coming from the left or right side, the kind of camera sensors on the sides of the car might not be as robust as the ones on the front of the self-driving car.

Yikes, it's like one of those old-time movies of the infamous "car stuck on the railroad tracks" dramatic scenes.

What maybe makes this worse is that at least a human driver might get other passengers out of the car.

Or, maybe the driver flags down another nearby car to help push their car off the tracks.

These are unlikely options for an AI self-driving car, at least for the foreseeable future.

I'll not dig more deeply into this specific use case herein, and suffice to say that it poses interesting and notably life-or-death consequences if it occurred.

There are numerous other kinds of edge cases that could be envisioned.

For example, suppose the railroad crossing gate comes down to warn that a train is coming. You've maybe seen this happen and then patiently waited for the arm to go up. Sometimes, a train doesn't come along, and yet the gate arm stays down.

This is obviously a dicey situation, since a human driver might be tempted to drive around the gate arm, first hopefully double-checking that there's no train within miles of eyesight.

What would a self-driving car do?

The odds are that most AI self-driving cars would dutifully sit there, stopped at the gate arm, and wait until doomsday since it assumes that it can only proceed once the gate arm goes up.

Again, the myriad of edge cases can all be eventually figured out, and I'm not suggesting that they are insurmountable.

The gist of the matter is that the current crop of AI self-driving cars that are gradually appearing on our public roadways have little if any depth of capability in dealing with railroad crossings. This is due to combination of lack of being programmed for it, along with the lack of sufficiently relevant training data for the Machine Learning and Deep Learning aspects of the AI system.

Conclusion

You might be familiar with the famous line that when you look in your sideview mirror, objects tend to be closer than they appear.

Equally notable is that trains are closer than they appear, and oftentimes are moving fast towards you, but from a head-on perspective the rate of closure is not completely apparent.

Though the number of train-vehicle crash deaths is small in comparison to car-on-car crash deaths, the stats show that you are thirty times more likely to die in a train-vehicle crash than a car-on-car crash.

This makes sense in that a train is a really big thing and your car is going to lose any kind of fight involving the train and vehicle hitting each other.

Please drive carefully when you come to railroad crossings.

Eventually, we'll have fully operational AI self-driving cars that have been robustly prepared for such matters, though in the meantime it is prudent to be wary about any so-called self-driving car that comes upon a railroad crossing. It's a tough hurdle to match to the everyday mantra of stop, look, and listen, even for AI.

CHAPTER 13

ROBOTS THAT DRIVE

AND

AI SELF-DRIVING CARS

CHAPTER 13

ROBOTS THAT DRIVE

AND

AI SELF-DRIVING CARS

Do you know a smarmy person that thinks they always have a better idea or a canny way to solve a vexing problem?

If so, you likely know how they often try to pop a balloon on existing approaches to solving things and offer a seemingly wholly new suggestion, somewhat out-of-the-blue, causing you to pause for thought about their eureka moment.

Let's consider the realm of self-driving cars.

There are billions upon billions of dollars being expended towards trying to design, develop, build, and field a true self-driving car.

True self-driving cars are ones that the AI drives the car entirely on its own and there isn't any human assistance during the driving task. These driverless cars are considered a Level 4 and Level 5, while a car that requires a human driver to co-share the driving effort is usually considered Level 2 and Level 3.

There is not as yet a true self-driving car at Level 5, which we don't yet even know if this will be possible to achieve, and nor how long it will take to get there. Meanwhile, the Level 4 efforts are gradually trying to get some traction by undergoing very narrow and selective public roadway trials, though there is controversy over whether this testing should be allowed per se (we are all life-or-death guinea pigs in an experiment taking place on our highways and byways, some point out).

So far, thousands of automotive engineers and AI developers have been toiling away at trying to invent a true self-driving car. Earlier claims that progress would be fast and sweet have shown to be over-hyped and unattainable.

If you consider this to be a vexing problem, and if you have a smarmy person that you know, they might ponder the matter and offer a seemingly out-of-the-box proposition.

Here's the bold idea: Rather than trying to build a self-driving car, why not instead just make a robot that can drive?

Well, by gosh, why didn't somebody think of that already, you might be wondering.

The answer is that it has been considered, and indeed there are some efforts trying to construct such a robot, but overall the belief is that we'll be more likely to sooner achieve self-driving cars via building driverless cars rather than trying to craft robots that can do the driving for us.

Let's unpack the matter, shall we?

The Beauty Of Having A Robot That Drives

Imagine if we had robots, the walking and talking type, and they could drive a car.

These are some of the benefits we'd derive:

- ***Conventional Cars Become Self-Driving.*** If you could have a robot sit in the driver's seat of any conventional car and be able to drive the vehicle, you'd be able to turn any and all conventional cars into being "self-driving" (well, they wouldn't need a human driver). That would be a huge plus. Right now, conventional cars generally need to be redesigned and built anew to be self-driving, leaving in the U.S. alone the 250 million conventional cars out-of-the-loop and ultimately headed to the scrapyard if people decide they'd rather get themselves a self-driving car (once such driverless cars arrive).

- ***Easily Switch Self-Driving From Car-To-Car.*** Presumably, you could have a robot driver that would readily be switched from driving one car to the next day driving a completely different car, merely by walking or carrying the robot to the driver's seat of the other car. With the design of the emerging self-driving cars, everything is built into the specific car and you can't somehow share it to suddenly make another car become self-driving.

- ***The Driver Would Be Seen.*** One of the qualms some have about the emerging self-driving cars is that there isn't a driver in the driver's seat, which is kind of eerie and worrisome since we are used to seeing someone sitting in that crucial position. The driver sitting there is reassuring in the sense that you know whether the car can possibly be driven, plus the driver can move their head and make eye contact to convey their driving intentions. Self-driving cars might have some kind of LED's or other displays to do similar signaling, but a robot with a robotic head would be even more familiar to us.

- **Could Use V2V, V2I, Etc.** Self-driving cars are being outfitted with V2V (vehicle-to-vehicle) electronic communications, allowing the AI of nearby cars to communicate with each other, and there will also be V2I (vehicle-to-infrastructure) involving the roadway signs and structures to electronically interact with driverless cars. If a human driver wanted to do V2V and V2I, it would be problematic since we humans aren't geared for direct electronic communications, but a robot driver would readily be able to do so.

- **Adjustable As Cars Advance.** Semi-autonomous cars are increasingly being loaded with ADAS (Advanced Driver-Assistance Systems), enabling automation to do more of the co-sharing driving effort with human drivers. In theory, a robot driver that was properly designed could easily be adjusted or updated via OTA (Over-The-Air) electronic downloads to be able to accommodate whatever new advances occur in the Level 2 and Level 3 cars. Your robot driver would then ascertain how much of the driving it will do versus how much it would let the ADAS do.

- **Invest In A Robot, Not In A Car.** There is an ongoing debate about the ownership of true self-driving cars, whereby some believe that only large corporations will own driverless cars and proffer them in fleets for ridesharing purposes. I am a contrarian and claim that we'll still have individuals owning such cars, but in any case, if you have a robot driver then potentially you wouldn't need to invest in a car per se. You might instead buy a robot driver and use it whenever you need to go for a ride, perhaps borrowing a friend's car, or using a ridesharing car that isn't yet driverless, and so on.

- *Reusable For Other Purposes.* A true self-driving car has pretty much one purpose, it is a car and used for transportation. A robot driver could be designed and built for doing lots of things, more so than merely driving a car. One of the worrisome issues about self-driving cars is that the "last mile" of doing actions like say delivering a package to someone's door is not feasible for the driverless car to do by itself. Potentially, a robot driver could get out of the car, on its own, and walk up to the door to deliver a package (these kinds of walking delivery robots are being built and tested today).

I've listed some of the handy advantages of pursuing a robot driver.

There are more aspects that arise as benefits, but let's not ignore the other side of the coin, namely the potential disadvantages or drawbacks.

No free lunch when it comes to the robot driver idea.

The Qualms About Having Robots That Drive

A robot driver is not necessarily a cure-all.

Consider this list of downsides about robot drivers:

- *Might Be Prone To Disrepair.* For a self-driving car, the guts of the tech are hidden within the car and hopefully going to work reliably. A robot driver that you are pulling into or out of a car is bound to get a lot of wear-and-tear. Do you really want a robot driver that is maybe in a state of disrepair driving your car? Don't think so.

- **Forces Cars To Remain As Designed Today.** Some believe that self-driving cars will have an entirely new interior and allow for human passengers to sleep, play, or work inside a car. This is partially possible due to the aspect that you can remove the driver's seat entirely, which is a fixed-in-place position that today that limits whatever else you might want to do with the design of the car interior. A robot driver would need to sit where today's human drivers sit; therefore, the car interior would still be burdened with a driver's seat.

- **That Frightening Feeling.** A robot sitting in the driver's seat is going to be quite chilling to see. Movie after movie has forewarned us of the day that robots take over our world. Even though having no visible driver might be eerie for truly self-driving cars, I'd bet that having a robot driving our cars will make people really bug out. Does society have the stomach for this or will humans' rebel once they see robots driving around town.

- **Hackers Delight.** There is worry that self-driving cars might get hacked, perhaps an evil programmer might plant a computer virus via using the OTA of the driverless car. It would seem perhaps even likelier that hacks would happen to a robot driver, more so than for true self-driving cars. The hacker can readily get ahold of a robot driver and try endlessly to crack into it. Doing the same for self-driving cars is going to be harder (though not impossible).

- **Robot Maintenance Looms.** When a car has troubles, you usually take it to an auto repair shop or a dealership. If your robot driver is having trouble, maybe the arms aren't working right or the robotic feet are slow to respond, where will you take it? We aren't yet ready to deal with thousands upon thousands of robots that need maintenance (maybe millions of them!), along with the repairs and replacement parts needed. It would be a significant undertaking to put in place such an infrastructure for robot driver upkeep.

- **_Safety Limitation Worries._** If you assume that the robot head is going to be somewhat akin to a human head, presumably the robot would have cameras as eyes and the visual component of the robot driver would be the mainstay of how it drives. Self-driving cars are being outfitted with cameras, along with radar, ultrasonic sensors, thermal imaging, LIDAR, and so on. Some believe that those other devices aren't needed since humans only use their eyes (mainly) to drive, but no one can say for sure that a robot driver using only visual elements could drive as well as a human. It might be worse.

- **_Other Concerns._** Maybe the robot driver weighs several hundred pounds, in which case it is not going to be so easy to switch it from car-to-car. The robot driver would presumably wear a seat belt, but how much movement would it be prepared to have? Might different seat belts and different kinds of driver's seats impact its ability to drive? Suppose the car takes a tight turn, will the robot driver stay in proper position to seamlessly continue driving the car? Lots of questions arise.

Those are just some of the issues that ensue when you consider the robot driver approach.

Conclusion

The consensus among self-driving car aficionados is that a robot driver is a long way away from being practical. A robot driver is considered generally to be more futuristic than trying to develop a self-driving car instead.

I'm not saying that we'll never have robot drivers.

There are some companies working on them today, along with research taking place in universities and labs.

Yet, one supposes that if we do achieve true self-driving cars, there might not be much of a need or value in having robot drivers, in which case we'll likely see robots that do other things but aren't particularly versed at driving. Of course, as mentioned earlier, robot drivers might take up the slack of being able to drive conventional cars, until eventually and presumably all conventional cars are weaned out of the stock of cars and self-driving cars become the nature of all cars.

You could also portray this as a moonshot-like race between the self-driving car makers and the robot driver makers.

If you could perfect robot drivers sooner than the perfection of self-driving cars, it would obviously put robot drivers into, well, the driver's seat.

Suppose too that true self-driving cars turned out to be impossible or infeasible, maybe the robot driver would provide an alternative that could be feasible.

No one knows.

Which then are you cheering for, the advent of self-driving cars or the emergence of robot drivers?

You might as well tell your smarmy friend that the notion of robot drivers is already underway, thus if the friend is irritatingly smarmy it's time to come up with another idea for solving the autonomous car problem.

Good luck with that.

CHAPTER 14

SMARTS OVER SPEED

AND

AI SELF-DRIVING CARS

CHAPTER 14

SMARTS OVER SPEED

AND

AI SELF-DRIVING CARS

It's the car duel of the century or some call it the skirmish at the Nurburgring racetrack.

I'm referring to the seemingly breathless competition that has been sparking the attention of car aficionados in pitting the newly unveiled Porsche Taycan, an EV sports car, against a Tesla.

Here's the sordid tale.

Porsche announced in early September their new EV sports car and showcased the Taycan's sportiness by providing its performance times based on racing around a legendary track, the Nurburgring in Germany, which is an especially demanding course and considered a purist dream track for both professional and amateur car racing.

Elon Musk then opted to prove the mettle of Tesla by having a modified Tesla Model S rocket around the Nurburgring racetrack, and eyewitnesses claim that the Model S readily bested the Taycan's recorded times by perhaps 20 seconds.

Right away, some said that the Tesla Model S breakneck time shouldn't yet count since it was not an "official" recording of trial time and thus it was merely based on (biased) eyewitness conjecture.

Furthermore, many have pointed out that the Tesla Model S had been demonstrably modified for the racetrack running and thus served as a contrived and outright unfair comparison to the Porsche Taycan that was a factory produced model.

The assertion is that an everyday off-the-production-line Tesla Model S should be used rather than a souped-up version.

The tussle continued when one of the Tesla Model S's being prepared for the racetrack happened to apparently breakdown midtrack and sat halted on the racetrack, meanwhile, by seeming coincidence, a Porsche Taycan drove past the stalled Tesla and a picture worth a thousand words was snapped.

The pic has become the talk of the town in that car buffs that are against Tesla point out the superiority of the Taycan that zipped past a dead-in-the-water Tesla Model S.

In any case, it is an easy bet that this macho drumbeating affair is going to continue unabated.

My car is faster than your car is the mantra of those that cherish their sporty vehicles.

One aspect to keep in mind and that often gets scant attention is that these racetrack times are not solely reflective of the car itself since it takes a human driver at the wheel to produce those racetrack shattering performances.

The person sitting in the driver's seat will make a significant difference in terms of how fast or how slow these sporty cars can complete the course.

I mention the role of the human driver because this sparks another point that might also be considered somewhat unspoken and hidden from view.

Here's the gist: *Should we be preoccupied with raw speed or would it be more fruitful to conduct car competitions focused on self-driving tech and how well one car compares to another as a self-driving car?*

In other words, maybe we are missing the boat by continuing to be excited about how fast cars can go, and instead, we ought to shift that enthusiasm and attention toward the future, namely the advent of true self-driving cars.

Let's unpack the matter.

Caring About Self-Driving Cars

Before launching into a heated debate about how to best compare tomorrow's state-of-the-art cars, it is important to clarify what I mean when using the phrase "self-driving cars" throughout this discussion.

There are semi-autonomous cars that require a human driver to be present and able to drive the car, doing so in a co-sharing arrangement with the automation of the car. These are often referred to as Level 2 and Level 3 cars and make use of ADAS (Advanced Driver-Assistance Systems).

Even more cutting-edge are the truly autonomous cars, ones that are self-driving and there is no human involved in the driving task. These driverless cars are considered at the Level 4 and Level 5 of self-driving autonomy (none fully exist as yet, and the roadway trials taking place are at best in the lower end of a Level 4).

A true self-driving car is one that meets the requirements of a truly autonomous car. Rather than repeatedly having to say the word "true" in front of the phrase self-driving car, just assume that a self-driving car is one that truly is autonomous.

For the semi-autonomous cars, the variety of ADAS features is quite expansive and there are essentially few if any standards governing how they work and what they do.

As such, trying to compare a car by automaker X that has its own set of ADAS is often hard to do in contrast to the ADAS of a car made by automaker Y. The differences are apt to be voluminous, plus each feature will have some positives and some negatives, making it problematic to say which is the better of the comparison.

I'm going to focus therefore on the notion of comparing self-driving cars rather than trying to compare semi-autonomous cars.

Your first thought might be that if a self-driving car is autonomous, shouldn't any and all self-driving cars simply drive in the same ways.

Sorry, that's not going to be the case.

Just as human drivers can drive cars in differing ways, so too will the AI driving systems be driving self-driving cars in differing ways.

Each automaker and tech firm that is developing a self-driving car are doing so in their own proprietary manner. This means that the driving style and approach for the various brands of self-driving cars will differ. In addition, it is likely that even the various models of a brand will be driving in differing ways.

I realize that this might seem like shocking news.

Many in the media seem to be suggesting that all AI driving systems are essentially cloned robots and will be driving in the same precise manner.

Not true.

As such, we now have a basis to consider an intriguing idea, perhaps we ought to be getting enamored about how AI driving systems are doing and showcase their "talents" by having them compete against each other, similar in a manner akin to comparing human-driven cars.

Competing Self-Driving Cars

The rapt attention that goes toward how fast cars can go is a business driver, one might say, pushing the automakers towards making faster and faster cars.

Yes, it's fun to talk about the speed that a car can take a given curve or zip down a straightway. There are bragging rights to be had. Buyers of cars are proud of their possibility of outgunning other cars on the roadway.

Of course, the reality is that most of the time you really are unable to fully exercise all that power under the hood of your car. Being stuck in commuter traffic does not especially highlight how fast your car can go and nor how quickly it can merge with other stop-and-go traffic.

You are sitting on top of an unleashed tiger, which may from time-to-time you get a chance to let loose, but most of the time it is caged and untapped.

Perhaps we should consider another direction rather than speed to push the automakers and tech firms toward.

Suppose we all got excited about the AI driving capabilities of self-driving cars.

Imagine if the news was filled with the latest breakthroughs of how a self-driving car navigated a dicey driving situation in a crowded downtown area. Or, how deftly a self-driving car managed to drive in a school drop-off zone and weaved safely around the crazy parents dropping off their children.

Instead of putting cars onto racetracks, perhaps we ought to be putting self-driving cars into proving grounds or closed tracks that are intended to test out AI driving capabilities, and then be excited about how those AI systems are doing there.

Indeed, the automakers and tech firms are already making use of proving grounds, yet it is something being done in a quiet manner and without any fanfare. Sure, it makes sense to be out of view when doing testing, and so it is certainly understandable that we don't hear much about it.

Once the self-driving car capabilities are mature enough, sufficient to be putting them onto our public roadways (which is a controversial act and some believe we are all guinea pigs in a dangerous ongoing public experiment), maybe we ought to become excited about comparing those self-driving cars on their closed track performances.

Metrics For Self-Driving Car Performance

It would be unseemly to focus on comparing self-driving cars solely by how fast they go, and thus we'll need to consider other factors of performance.

I'm not suggesting that the AI shouldn't ultimately be able to drive fast, which is fine when appropriately undertaken.

Let's though first aim at driving legally and safely, and we can then come back around to the speed factor later.

We'll need to be interested in the more mundane acts of driving that we all take for granted.

Everyday driving such as:

- How soon did a self-driving car detect and avoid a pedestrian that was jaywalking?
- Did the self-driving car merge with human-driven cars in a manner that kept the traffic flowing?
- Was the AI able to drive in a cramped parking lot that had lots of cars and people, and did it do so without bumping into anyone or anything?
- Etc.

One of the issues facing the advent of self-driving cars is that there are not yet any accepted standards about what constitutes a safe and road-ready self-driving car.

Currently, the automakers and tech firms that are building self-driving cars can pretty much decide whether they believe that their driverless cars are road-ready or not.

Most of the time, a human back-up driver is included in the self-driving car as it is undertaking public roadway tryouts, though having a human back-up driver does not guarantee the avoidance of crashes (as per the famous Uber incident in Arizona).

Thus, it is in the eye of the beholder as to whether a self-driving car is ready for prime time.

Some believe that this is too loosey-goosey and we are going to regret not having established a kind of Turing Test for self-driving cars (for my article on this topic, use this link).

Conclusion

Overall, the point herein is that instead of being overly preoccupied with the pursuit of fast rides, it might be handy and helpful to refocus some of our energies toward self-driving cars and a future of automated driving.

This reminds me of the famous joke about the man in a parking lot at nighttime that is furtively looking for his lost car keys, doing so under the light emanating from an adjacent light post.

Another person comes along and offers to help look for the keys.

After a few moments of combined searching, the helper asks where the keys were approximately dropped. The man points toward a distant and darkened area of the parking lot and says that he dropped the keys over there.

Perplexed that they aren't searching in the darkened area, the helper asks why then they are searching in a spot that is unlikely to be hiding the keys. The man brashly offers that it's because this is where the light is.

Drum roll, please.

Perhaps we're right now looking at the speed of cars because that's where the light happens to be shining, but we ought to be looking where the keys really are, namely residing in the advent of self-driving cars.

Don't interpret this proposition to mean that we can't still have fun about human-driven cars and how fast they can go.

Presumably, even once we have widespread AI-driven cars, the odds are that we humans will still be fascinated by the incredibly fast driving of human-driven cars.

Far off in the future, it is forecast by some pundits that we won't have any human-driven cars at all. In which case, maybe we'll be going to racetracks to watch AI systems driving self-driving cars at breathtaking speeds, rather than seeing human drivers do so.

Or, we might have racetracks that specialize in the old-time human-driven approach and for the sake of tradition allow humans to drive sporty cars. The populous at large might have decided that human drivers should never be on public streets, but if human drivers want to drive around a "silly" racetrack, so be it.

There are some that believe we'll never reach a time when we'll ban all human driving from our roadways and that a mix of AI-driven cars and human-driven cars will always be allowed.

For now, we're bound to continue to compare racetrack times of one car versus another, and perhaps we'll gradually get equally excited about how one brand of self-driving car did a greater job at everyday driving than did a competing brand.

I'll make a champagne toast to that moonshot race-winning feat for self-driving cars.

CHAPTER 15

HAVOC RATINGS

AND

AI SELF-DRIVING CARS

CHAPTER 15

HAVOC RATINGS

AND

AI SELF-DRIVING CARS

The football season is well underway.

One of the more unusual and lesser-known metrics for analyzing football teams consists of their havoc rating.

Havoc ratings are increasingly being quoted and discussed, along with being used as a motivational tool by football coaches that want to get their team pumped-up and cognizant of how the team is doing.

What is a havoc rating?

Simply stated, you count up the number of football plays that your defense was able to disrupt the opposing team, such as plays when your defense was able to intercept the football, or forced the opposing team to fumble the ball, or tackled the opposing side for a loss of yardage.

Next, you divide that count of disrupted plays by the total number of plays undertaken by the opposing team.

The resulting fraction is turned into a percentage, allowing you to readily see what percentage of the time that the defense was able to mess-up the opposing side's offense.

For example, if there were 100 plays by the opposing team and your defense was able to undermine the offense on 25 of those plays, you would have a havoc rating of 25% (that's 25 divided by 100).

Essentially, the havoc rating reflects how well your defense can create havoc upon the opposing side.

The opposing side wants to keep the havoc rating as low as possible, suggesting that they don't allow themselves to be disrupted.

Meanwhile, the defense is aiming to get as high a havoc rating as they can, showcasing how often they are able to cause the offense to slip-up.

If you had a havoc rating of 100%, it would mean that on every play that was run by the opposing team, you managed to confound their efforts. That would be tremendous as a defense. Of course, if you had a havoc rating of zero, it would suggest that your defense is not doing its job and that the opposing side is making plays without being at all disturbed or undermined.

Kirby Smart, the football coach for the Georgia Bulldogs (college team of the University of Georgia), adamantly believes in the value of calculating and using the havoc rating. He is widely known for having his football players recite by heart the latest havoc rating of the Bulldogs and be able to explain what it is and how it is trending, doing so at each practice session.

Just recently, the Bulldogs bested Notre Dame, considered a tremendous upset, and perhaps the team's awareness of "havoc" provided inspiration to then during the tense and exhilarating match-up.

Havoc ratings can be used in other endeavors too.

One modest proposal is that perhaps we ought to be using a havoc rating when it comes to the emergence of true self-driving cars.

On the surface, you might be puzzled that havoc has anything whatsoever to do with self-driving cars.

Let's unpack the matter and see.

Understanding Havoc And Self-Driving Cars

True self-driving cars are ones that the AI drives the car entirely on its own and there isn't any human assistance during the driving task.

These driverless cars are considered a Level 4 and Level 5, while a car that requires a human driver to co-share the driving effort is usually considered at a Level 2 or Level 3. The cars that co-share the driving task are considered semi-autonomous, and typically contain a variety of automated add-ons that are referred to as ADAS (Advanced Driver-Assistance Systems).

There is not yet a true self-driving car at Level 5, which we don't yet even know if this will be possible to achieve, and nor how long it will take to get there.

Meanwhile, the Level 4 efforts are gradually trying to get some traction by undergoing very narrow and selective public roadway trials, though there is controversy over whether this testing should be allowed per se (we are all life-or-death guinea pigs in an experiment taking place on our highways and byways, some point out).

Since the semi-autonomous cars require a human driver, I'm not going to try and apply a havoc rating to the efforts of a Level 2 or Level 3 car. We could do so, but it would make the havoc aspects murky because there would be a portion attributable to the human driver and another portion caused by the automation, likely a blur of the two sources.

Instead, let's focus on the havoc aspects involving true self-driving cars, ones at Level 4 and Level 5. With the AI being the only driver, the havoc aspects can be assigned to the driving system per se.

There are two ways in which havoc can arise:
1) By the actions of human drivers and for which the AI must contend
2) By the action of the AI driving system and for which other drivers need to contend

I think that we would all agree that human drivers often create havoc in traffic. As such, it is important that the AI driving system be able to cope with havoc instigated by nearby human drivers.

You might be somewhat surprised at the second way in which havoc arises, namely by the actions of the AI driving system. Many pundits claim that AI driving systems will be perfect drivers, but as you'll see in a moment, this is a false and misleading assumption.

Before I jump into the fray, there are pundits that also assert that we'll have only self-driving cars on our roadways and therefore there isn't a need to deal with human drivers. Only someone living in a dream world would believe that we are only going to have self-driving cars and won't also have human drivers in other nearby cars.

In the United States alone, there are about 250 million conventional cars. All those cars are not going to suddenly be dispatched to the scrap heap upon the introduction of self-driving cars. For a lengthy foreseeable future, there will be both human-driven cars and self-driving cars mixing together on our highways and byways.

It stands to reason.

Human Drivers Create Havoc

Consider the apparent notion that human drivers can create havoc.

You are driving along, minding your own business, when a car that's to your left opts to dart in front of your car and make a right turn at the corner up ahead.

We've all experienced that kind of panicky and curse invoking driving situation.

The lout that shockingly performs such a dangerous driving act is creating havoc.

They are likely to disrupt your driving, forcing you to heavily use your brakes, maybe even causing you to swerve to avoid hitting their car. A car behind you might then need to also take radical actions, trying to avoid you, while you are trying to avoid the transgressor.

There might be pedestrians standing at the corner that see the madcap car heading toward them, forcing them to leap away and cower on the sidewalk.

Imagine then a human driver that over the course of a driving journey might undertake some number of havocs producing driving actions. Divide the number of havoc acts by the total number of overall driving actions, and you have a percentage that reveals their havoc rating.

The higher a havoc rating for a driver, the worse a driver they are. For a driver with a low havoc rating, it tends to suggest that they are not creating untoward driving circumstances while on the public roadways.

Are you already thinking about a friend or colleague that you are sure must have a sky-high havoc rating?

I'm sure you know such driving Neanderthals.

Currently, few of the self-driving cars that are being tried out on our roadways are particularly versed in dealing with high havoc-rated human drivers.

Most of the self-driving cars generally assume that the traffic around them will be relatively calm and mundane. You can think of those self-driving cars as acting a bit like a timid teenage driver that is just starting to drive a car. Those novice drivers hope and pray that no other driver will do something outlandish.

If other drivers do crazy things, the teenage driver will resort to the simplest possible retort, which might be applicable or might make the situation even worse. In the case of getting cut off by the driver to their left that is darting toward a right turn, the novice driver might jam on the brakes and come to a sudden halt. Doing so might not have been the best choice, and it could end up with the car behind them rear-ending their car.

True self-driving cars need to step-up their game and be able to contend with high havoc human drivers.

This capability can either be hand programmed into the AI driving system or can be "learned" overtime via the use of Machine Learning (ML) and Deep Learning (DL). I don't want to though suggest that the ML and DL are equivalent to human learning, which they most decidedly are not. There is no kind of common-sense reasoning involved in today's ML and DL, nor do I expect to see such a capability anytime soon.

Self-Driving Cars Create Havoc

Now that we've covered the obvious use case of human drivers that create havoc, let's explore the lesser realized aspect that self-driving cars can also generate havoc.

Suppose that a true self-driving car is coming down the street. The self-driving car is moving along at the posted speed limit and obeying all the local traffic laws.

A pedestrian on the sidewalk is looking at their smartphone and not paying attention to the traffic, and nor noticing the sidewalk activity since their nose is pointed at their phone.

Oops, the distracted pedestrian nearly walks right into a fire hydrant. At the last moment, the pedestrian sidesteps around the fire hydrant, moving suddenly onto the curb.

The AI driving system of the self-driving car is using its cameras, radar, LIDAR, ultrasonic sensors, and other detection devices to monitor the traffic and nearby pedestrians.

Upon detecting the pedestrian that seems to be bent on entering into the street, and not realizing that the pedestrian was merely avoiding conking into a fire hydrant, the AI calculates that the pedestrian might get into harm's way and end-up in front of the car.

Wanting to be as safe as possible, the AI instructs the car to come to an immediate halt.

Well, it turns out that the sudden stop of the self-driving car then leads to a human-driven car that is behind the driverless car to rear-end the self-driving car.

The point is that the actions of the AI driving system can be well-intended (though don't ascribe human intention to the AI system, please, at least until someday the "singularity" happens), and yet the efforts produce havoc.

Similar in some respects to the earlier description of a novice teenage driver, the AI system is going to be performing driving acts that have as an adverse consequence the generation of havoc.

Thus, perhaps we ought to be measuring the havoc ratings of self-driving cars.

Conclusion

A driverless car that has a high havoc rating should either be prevented from driving around or at least shunted into specific driving areas whereby the havoc producing actions won't have serious consequences (such as when moving at very low speeds or driving in lanes devoted exclusively to self-driving cars).

I realize that some of you might be exclaiming that the havoc producing self-driving car can readily be updated with better software by undertaking an OTA (Over-The-Air) electronic communications and downloading improved driving AI.

Yes, that's true, but you are also mistakenly assuming that somehow those changes are going to be immediately ready and usable.

Not so.

Gradually, over time, presumably, the AI driving systems will be improved.

Meanwhile, we are going to be somewhat at the mercy of whatever havoc producing AI driving systems are on our roadways.

Allow me to quote from Shakespeare (Act 3, Scene 1): "Cry 'Havoc!,' and let slip the dogs of war."

This famous line from the play *Julius Caesar* is spoken by Mark Antony and indicates that he wanted to go after the assassins that murdered Caesar.

The dogs of war are most likely actual dogs that were trained for warfare and he was saying that the killer dogs should be let loose to attack the assassins, though the expression might also mean to let loose the military forces overall.

For the self-driving cars that are currently being let loose on our roadways, and once they no longer have back-up human drivers attending to the driving of the AI system, will we be potentially incurring havoc and will those AI systems be able to also contend with the havoc created by human drivers?

Nobody knows, and especially nobody knows if we aren't measuring the havoc producing and havoc handling capabilities of self-driving cars.

Automakers and tech firms might be well-intended in their spirited efforts to get self-driving cars onto our roads, but let's not also allow ourselves to fall into the trap of unleashing havoc.

I think Shakespeare, if he were alive today, would likely have something to say about that.

CHAPTER 16

SEX-ON-WHEELS

AND

AI SELF-DRIVING CARS

CHAPTER 16

SEX-ON-WHEELS

AND

AI SELF-DRIVING CARS

What happens inside self-driving cars will stay inside self-driving cars.

Maybe.

A recent online ad posted by a major automaker caused quite a stir because the emphasis was about an amorous couple that was seemingly doing something, uh, let's say amorous, while inside a self-driving car.

We don't have true self-driving cars yet, so this ad was about a potential future.

The ad was taken down after a brouhaha arose.

To prevent your imagination from running wild about the video, please be aware that the racy clip was not X-rated. Instead, the brief video was cleverly cut together to imply that (per the ad) "new moments of joy" are on our horizon.

Some were offended by the implication that advances in self-driving tech would be sullied by being associated with the most basic and puritan forms of human affection.

Here's an interesting question: *Will the advent of true self-driving cars lead us toward an era of sex-on-wheels?*

Let's unpack the matter.

Self-Driving Cars Explained

First, I'll clarify what I mean when referring to true self-driving cars.

True self-driving cars are ones that the AI drives the car entirely on its own and there isn't any human assistance during the driving task.

These driverless cars are considered a Level 4 and Level 5, while a car that requires a human driver to co-share the driving effort is usually considered at a Level 2 or Level 3. The cars that co-share the driving task are described as being semi-autonomous, and typically contain a variety of automated add-ons that are coined as ADAS (Advanced Driver-Assistance Systems).

There is not yet a true self-driving car at Level 5, which we don't yet even know if this will be possible to achieve, and nor how long it will take to get there.

Meanwhile, the Level 4 efforts are gradually trying to get some traction by undergoing very narrow and selective public roadway trials, though there is controversy over whether this testing should be allowed per se (we are all life-or-death guinea pigs in an experiment taking place on our highways and byways, some point out).

Since the semi-autonomous cars require a human driver, I'm not going to consider them as an enclave for amorous activity. There is essentially no difference between trying to be amorous in a Level 2 or Level 3 car than it is to do so inside a conventional car.

It is notable to point out that in spite of those dolts that keep posting videos of themselves falling asleep at the wheel of a Level 2 or Level 3 car, do not be misled into believing that you can take away your attention from the driving task while driving a semi-autonomous car.

You are the responsible party for the driving actions of the car, regardless of how much automation might be tossed into a Level 2 or Level 3.

There have been some videos of a driver performing amorous activities while at the wheel, but those are either faked videos or worse still they are videos showcasing outlandish driving and endangerment of those inside the car and any nearby cars or pedestrians.

Busted.

Let's then focus on the amorous aspects involving passengers inside true self-driving cars, ones at Level 4 and Level 5.

With the AI being the driver, there are only passengers inside a true self-driving car.

Private Enclave Inside A Self-Driving Car

There are some handy advantages to removing human drivers from cars.

Besides the hoped-for belief that the number of car crashes will be reduced, there is also the subtle but significant aspect that the interior of the car can be redesigned.

Many anticipate that the inside of self-driving cars will become an open area that allows for people to no longer be forced into fixed seated positions that are locked into looking forward.

Some concept cars showcase several swivel seats, allowing passengers to face in whatever direction they wish to do so. You can face forward in the conventional manner, or face to the back of the car, or spin around if that's your cup of tea.

You can face others that are also seated in the self-driving car, potentially sharing stories and having a good time, or perhaps carrying on serious work in a group setting, doing so while the AI is driving the car for you all.

Many expect that we will oftentimes opt to take naps while inside a self-driving car.

If your commute to work takes an hour each way, perhaps you can get some extra sleep in the morning on the way to work and catch another nap on the way back home in the evening. The swivel seats might recline for sleeping, or perhaps there are beds that can tilt up.

The windows of self-driving cars might also be transformed.

Some believe that there won't be any windows at all. Instead, the interior will be completely lined with LED displays. You can then watch your favorite streaming movies while going for a ride. You might take an online course offered by a remote college.

If you want to look outside, the LED displays will show you what the cameras that are mounted on the outside of the car are seeing. Those cameras are there primarily for the AI system to detect the roadway, but you can tap into the cameras if you want to see the outside world too.

Advances in window technology are likely to allow for a type of glass that can be switched from being opaque to transparent. Thus, rather than removing the windows from self-driving cars, you'll be able to press a button and use the windows to see outside, and another press of the button to make them opaque and used as an LED display inside the self-driving car.

Let's piece together the facts:

- No human driver

- Interior opened up

- Beds or recliner seats for sleeping

- Windows can be darkened

What does that add up to?

For some, it means time to party.

You don't need to worry about the driving task and can put your attention toward other tasks.

For teenagers, the adult driver that usually sits in the car and dampens your chances of partying, well, there isn't an adult driver seated in a self-driving car.

No witness.

Trying to have amorous activities inside a conventional car can be physically challenging due to the layout of the seats. In a self-driving car, the odds are that beds or the equivalent are intentionally included.

In sum, you have what seems to be a private enclave.

Yes, this could certainly prompt people to employ their most primitive instincts.

When you glance at that self-driving car on the freeway that is adjacent to your car, you'll have no direct way to know what might be happening inside that self-driving car.

Perhaps some freeway fun is taking place.

I realize that with today's vans or even some SUVs, the same kind of activity could be taking place, though this is rather limited and generally rare.

Once we have a preponderance of self-driving cars on our highways and byways, the acts of desire inside those self-driving cars might be taking place all the time and anywhere that the self-driving cars are being deployed.

Furthermore, think about teenagers and their hormones.

Your teenager takes the family self-driving car to school, doing so without adult supervision inside the driverless car. The teenager tells the AI system to stop at a friend's house to pick-up a fellow student.

After getting into the self-driving car, the two decide to perform some hanky-panky.

The teenager might even tell the AI to take the long route to school, providing some added time to undertake the encounter (yes, the AI could become an accomplice to the act).

In case you are thinking that such a scenario would be unlikely, I dare say that the peer pressure among teenagers is quite fierce and providing them with a private enclave is likely to start a forest fire if you know what I mean.

Parents Worst Nightmare

Those of you that might be or become parents in an era of self-driving cars, the advent of self-driving cars offers some interesting challenges.

There's actually a relatively simple way to put a stop to the private opportunities that might occur inside self-driving cars, namely undermine the privacy aspects.

Here's what I mean.

Pundits predict that most self-driving cars will be used for ridesharing or ride-hailing. This makes sense and offers a tremendous upside of having mobility available 24 x 7.

One can anticipate that the owners of these driverless cars will want to know that the passengers aren't ripping up the seats and upholstery to shreds. Unlike today's Uber or Lyft that have human drivers, acting as protectors of the car, there won't be any human driver sitting inside self-driving cars.

The automakers and tech firms are going to be outfitting the interior of self-driving cars with cameras that face inward into the car. This allows for video recording of what takes place and can even be used to watch in real-time the activities taking place inside the driverless car.

We can revisit the situation of the parent that sends their teenager to school in the family self-driving car.

Sitting at home, the parent waves goodbye as the teenager is whisked along by the driverless car. The parent brings up on their smartphone the camera that points to the interior of the self-driving car. Using a real-time interactive link, the parent talks face-to-face remotely with the teenager and double-checks that the teenager did their homework last night.

When the teenager has the self-driving car pick-up their friend, the parent might say hello, plus the parent of the friend might join the conversation.

Those teenagers would seem unlikely to undertake taboo activities.

Sure, they might try to be tricky and cover the cameras, but this would not be especially viable under the gaze of the parents and I'd bet that when those kids get home there will be heck to pay.

As an added twist, imagine the teenager pleading beforehand with their parent to not use the cameras that are inside the self-driving car. Don't you trust me? If you really trusted me, you would not turn-on the cameras.

My sympathies for those parents in the era of self-driving cars.

One other added aspect involves the AI system.

It might be difficult or time consuming for parents to watch their kids while those children are on driverless car journeys. With sophisticated AI, the AI system could become a nanny or overseer.

The AI system would be examining the video being captured of the interior of the car. If untoward actions are detected, the AI might warn the passengers, or possibly send an alert to a parent.

This same kind of AI watchfulness will likely be used by ridesharing firms that have fleets of self-driving cars.

Having to hire labor that would be watching the fleet and trying to detect what activities are taking place would be expensive and a logistic nightmare. Just use the AI to catch most of it, and then perhaps have handfuls of humans that connect when the AI is unsure of what is happening.

Conclusion

We've kind of dashed the hopes of amorous efforts while inside self-driving cars.

Not really.

Suppose you own a self-driving car and can decide whether to have the cameras activated or not. In that case, you can carry on your own acts and not worry that someone could be watching.

For a ridesharing service, perhaps they might offer for an added price that they will turn off the cameras.

These premium costing self-driving cars allow adults to be adults.

Or, depending again on your cup of tea, maybe the cameras are kept on, allowing a taping of the events that occur. In a more extravagant way, the cameras of self-driving cars around the globe could share with each other, for those that sign-up for a special service offering those kinds of connections.

Rolling hayrides, in a sense.

Of course, being inside a moving car and not wearing a seatbelt is dangerous.

That might curtail some activity, on the other hand, there are new advances being researched to make other kinds of vehicle constraints that offer more freedom of movement for self-driving car passengers.

Some locales today don't allow the windows of a car to hide seeing into the interior.

Might we have laws that say that self-driving cars will not be allowed to block their windows, partially to try and prevent private actions that might otherwise take place inside a driverless car?

As with any new innovation, there are lots of nuances that have yet to be ascertained.

One thing that we do know is that humans have primal instincts, and advances in self-driving cars aren't going to somehow stop those instincts.

You might contend that self-driving cars could fuel those instincts. Could the advent of self-driving cars ultimately be correlated to birthrates?

That's something to think about.

APPENDIX

APPENDIX A

TEACHING WITH THIS MATERIAL

The material in this book can be readily used either as a supplemental to other content for a class, or it can also be used as a core set of textbook material for a specialized class. Classes where this material is most likely used include any classes at the college or university level that want to augment the class by offering thought provoking and educational essays about AI and self-driving cars.

In particular, here are some aspects for class use:

o   <u>Computer Science</u>. Studying AI, autonomous vehicles, etc.

o   <u>Business</u>. Exploring technology and it adoption for business.

o   <u>Sociology</u>. Sociological views on the adoption and advancement of technology.

Specialized classes at the undergraduate and graduate level can also make use of this material.

For each chapter, consider whether you think the chapter provides material relevant to your course topic. There is plenty of opportunity to get the students thinking about the topic and force them to decide whether they agree or disagree with the points offered and positions taken. I would also encourage you to have the students do additional research beyond the chapter material presented (I provide next some suggested assignments they can do).

RESEARCH ASSIGNMENTS ON THESE TOPICS

Your students can find background material on these topics, doing so in various business and technical publications. I list below the top ranked AI related journals. For business publications, I would suggest the usual culprits such as the Harvard Business Review, Forbes, Fortune, WSJ, and the like.

Here are some suggestions of homework or projects that you could assign to students:

a) <u>Assignment for foundational AI research topic</u>: Research and prepare a paper and a presentation on a specific aspect of Deep AI, Machine Learning, ANN, etc. The paper should cite at least 3 reputable sources. Compare and contrast to what has been stated in this book.

b) <u>Assignment for the Self-Driving Car topic</u>: Research and prepare a paper and Self-Driving Cars. Cite at least 3 reputable sources and analyze the characterizations. Compare and contrast to what has been stated in this book.

c) <u>Assignment for a Business topic</u>: Research and prepare a paper and a presentation on businesses and advanced technology. What is hot, and what is not? Cite at least 3 reputable sources. Compare and contrast to the depictions in this book.

d) <u>Assignment to do a Startup:</u> Have the students prepare a paper about how they might startup a business in this realm. They must submit a sound Business Plan for the startup. They could also be asked to present their Business Plan and so should also have a presentation deck to coincide with it.

You can certainly adjust the aforementioned assignments to fit to your particular needs and the class structure. You'll notice that I ask for 3 reputable cited sources for the paper writing based assignments. I usually steer students toward "reputable" publications, since otherwise they will cite some oddball source that has no credentials other than that they happened to write something and post it onto the Internet. You can define "reputable" in whatever way you prefer, for example some faculty think Wikipedia is not reputable while others believe it is reputable and allow students to cite it.

The reason that I usually ask for at least 3 citations is that if the student only does one or two citations they usually settle on whatever they happened to find the fastest. By requiring three citations, it usually seems to force them to look around, explore, and end-up probably finding five or more, and then whittling it down to 3 that they will actually use.

I have not specified the length of their papers, and leave that to you to tell the students what you prefer. For each of those assignments, you could end-up with a short one to two pager, or you could do a dissertation length paper. Base the length on whatever best fits for your class, and the credit amount of the assignment within the context of the other grading metrics you'll be using for the class.

I mention in the assignments that they are to do a paper and prepare a presentation. I usually try to get students to present their work. This is a good practice for what they will do in the business world. Most of the time, they will be required to prepare an analysis and present it. If you don't have the class time or inclination to have the students present, then you can of course cut out the aspect of them putting together a presentation.

If you want to point students toward highly ranked journals in AI, here's a list of the top journals as reported by *various citation counts sources* (this list changes year to year):

- o   Communications of the ACM
- o   Artificial Intelligence
- o   Cognitive Science
- o   IEEE Transactions on Pattern Analysis and Machine Intelligence
- o   Foundations and Trends in Machine Learning
- o   Journal of Memory and Language
- o   Cognitive Psychology
- o   Neural Networks
- o   IEEE Transactions on Neural Networks and Learning Systems
- o   IEEE Intelligent Systems
- o   Knowledge-based Systems

GUIDE TO USING THE CHAPTERS

For each of the chapters, I provide next some various ways to use the chapter material. You can assign the tasks as individual homework assignments, or the tasks can be used with team projects for the class. You can easily layout a series of assignments, such as indicating that the students are to do item "a" below for say Chapter 1, then "b" for the next chapter of the book, and so on.

a) What is the main point of the chapter and describe in your own words the significance of the topic,

b) Identify at least two aspects in the chapter that you agree with, and support your concurrence by providing at least one other outside researched item as support; make sure to explain your basis for disagreeing with the aspects,

c) Identify at least two aspects in the chapter that you disagree with, and support your disagreement by providing at least one other outside researched item as support; make sure to explain your basis for disagreeing with the aspects,

d) Find an aspect that was not covered in the chapter, doing so by conducting outside research, and then explain how that aspect ties into the chapter and what significance it brings to the topic,

e) Interview a specialist in industry about the topic of the chapter, collect from them their thoughts and opinions, and readdress the chapter by citing your source and how they compared and contrasted to the material,

f) Interview a relevant academic professor or researcher in a college or university about the topic of the chapter, collect from them their thoughts and opinions, and readdress the chapter by citing your source and how they compared and contrasted to the material,

g) Try to update a chapter by finding out the latest on the topic, and ascertain whether the issue or topic has now been solved or whether it is still being addressed, explain what you come up with.

The above are all ways in which you can get the students of your class involved in considering the material of a given chapter. You could mix things up by having one of those above assignments per each week, covering the chapters over the course of the semester or quarter.

As a reminder, here are the chapters of the book and you can select whichever chapters you find most valued for your particular class:

<u>Chapter Title</u>

1   Eliot Framework for AI Self-Driving Cars

2   Roadkill and AI Self-Driving Cars

3   Safe Driver Cities and AI Self-Driving Cars

4   Tailgate Parties and AI Self-Driving Cars

5   Tesla's AI Chips and AI Self-Driving Cars

6   Elites-Only and AI Self-Driving Cars

7   Four Year Lifecycle and AI Self-Driving Cars

8   Entrepreneurs and AI Self-Driving Cars

9   Autopilot Crash Lessons and AI Self-Driving Cars

10   U.N. Framework and AI Self-Driving Cars

11   Sports Cars and AI Self-Driving Cars

12   Railroad Crossings and AI Self-Driving Cars

13   Robots That Drive and AI Self-Driving Car

14   Smarts Over Speed and AI Self-Driving Cars

15   Havoc Ratings and AI Self-Driving Cars

16   Sex-on-Wheels and AI Self-Driving Cars

Companion Book By This Author

Advances in AI and Autonomous Vehicles: Cybernetic Self-Driving Cars

Practical Advances in Artificial Intelligence (AI) and Machine Learning

by

Dr. Lance B. Eliot, MBA, PhD

This title is available via Amazon and other book sellers

<u>Companion Book By This Author</u>

Self-Driving Cars:
"The Mother of All AI Projects"

by Dr. Lance B. Eliot, MBA, PhD

<u>Chapter Title</u>

This title is available via Amazon and other book sellers

Companion Book By This Author

Innovation and Thought Leadership on Self-Driving Driverless Cars

by Dr. Lance B. Eliot, MBA, PhD

This title is available via Amazon and other book sellers

<u>Companion Book By This Author</u>

New Advances in AI Autonomous Driverless Cars Self-Driving Cars

by Dr. Lance B. Eliot, MBA, PhD

This title is available via Amazon and other book sellers

Companion Book By This Author

Introduction to
Driverless Self-Driving Cars

by Dr. Lance B. Eliot, MBA, PhD

This title is available via Amazon and other book sellers

Companion Book By This Author

Autonomous Vehicle Driverless
Self-Driving Cars and Artificial Intelligence

by Dr. Lance B. Eliot, MBA, PhD

This title is available via Amazon and other book sellers

Companion Book By This Author

Transformative Artificial Intelligence Driverless Self-Driving Cars

by Dr. Lance B. Eliot, MBA, PhD

This title is available via Amazon and other book sellers

Companion Book By This Author

*Disruptive Artificial Intelligence
and Driverless Self-Driving Cars*

by Dr. Lance B. Eliot, MBA, PhD

This title is available via Amazon and other book sellers

Companion Book By This Author

State-of-the-Art
AI Driverless Self-Driving Cars

by Dr. Lance B. Eliot, MBA, PhD

Chapter Title

This title is available via Amazon and other book sellers

.

Top Trends in AI Self-Driving Cars

by Dr. Lance B. Eliot, MBA, PhD

Chapter Title

This title is available via Amazon and other book sellers

Companion Book By This Author

AI Innovations and Self-Driving Cars

by Dr. Lance B. Eliot, MBA, PhD

Chapter Title

1 Eliot Framework for AI Self-Driving Cars

2 API's and Self-Driving Cars

3 Egocentric Designs and Self-Driving Cars

4 Family Road Trip and Self-Driving Cars

5 AI Developer Burnout and Tesla Car Crash

6 Stealing Secrets About Self-Driving Cars

7 Affordability and Self-Driving Cars

8 Crossing the Rubicon and Self-Driving Cars

9 Addicted to Self-Driving Cars

10 Ultrasonic Harm and Self-Driving Cars

11 Accidents Contagion and Self-Driving Cars

12 Non-Stop 24x7 and Self-Driving Cars

13 Human Life Spans and Self-Driving Cars

This title is available via Amazon and other book sellers

Companion Book By This Author

Crucial Advances for
AI Self-Driving Cars

by Dr. Lance B. Eliot, MBA, PhD

This title is available via Amazon and other book sellers

<u>Companion Book By This Author</u>

Sociotechnical Insights and AI Driverless Cars

by Dr. Lance B. Eliot, MBA, PhD

<u>Chapter Title</u>

This title is available via Amazon and other book sellers

Companion Book By This Author

Pioneering Advances for
AI Driverless Cars

by Dr. Lance B. Eliot, MBA, PhD

This title is available via Amazon and other book sellers

Companion Book By This Author

Leading Edge Trends for AI Driverless Cars

by Dr. Lance B. Eliot, MBA, PhD

Chapter Title

This title is available via Amazon and other book sellers

<u>Companion Book By This Author</u>

The Cutting Edge of AI Autonomous Cars

by Dr. Lance B. Eliot, MBA, PhD

<u>Chapter Title</u>

This title is available via Amazon and other book sellers

<u>Companion Book By This Author</u>

The Next Wave of
AI Self-Driving Cars

by Dr. Lance B. Eliot, MBA, PhD

<u>Chapter Title</u>

This title is available via Amazon and other book sellers

Companion Book By This Author

Revolutionary Innovations of AI Self-Driving Cars

by Dr. Lance B. Eliot, MBA, PhD

Chapter Title

This title is available via Amazon and other book sellers

Companion Book By This Author

AI Self-Driving Cars
Breakthroughs

by Dr. Lance B. Eliot, MBA, PhD

Chapter Title

This title is available via Amazon and other book sellers

Companion Book By This Author

Trailblazing Trends for AI Self-Driving Cars

by Dr. Lance B. Eliot, MBA, PhD

Chapter Title

This title is available via Amazon and other book sellers

Companion Book By This Author

Ingenious Strides for
AI Driverless Cars

by Dr. Lance B. Eliot, MBA, PhD

Chapter Title

This title is available via Amazon and other book sellers

Companion Book By This Author

AI Self-Driving Cars
Inventiveness

by Dr. Lance B. Eliot, MBA, PhD

This title is available via Amazon and other book sellers

Companion Book By This Author

Visionary Secrets of AI Driverless Cars

by Dr. Lance B. Eliot, MBA, PhD

Chapter Title

This title is available via Amazon and other book sellers

<u>Companion Book By This Author</u>

Spearheading
AI Self-Driving Cars

by Dr. Lance B. Eliot, MBA, PhD

<u>Chapter Title</u>

This title is available via Amazon and other book sellers

Companion Book By This Author

Spurring
AI Self-Driving Cars

by Dr. Lance B. Eliot, MBA, PhD

This title is available via Amazon and other book sellers

Avant-Garde
AI Driverless Cars

by Dr. Lance B. Eliot, MBA, PhD

Chapter Title

AI Self-Driving Cars
Evolvement

by Dr. Lance B. Eliot, MBA, PhD

Chapter Title

This title is available via Amazon and other book sellers

Companion Book By This Author

AI Driverless Cars
Chrysalis

by Dr. Lance B. Eliot, MBA, PhD

This title is available via Amazon and other book sellers

<u>Companion Book By This Author</u>

Boosting
AI Autonomous Cars
by Dr. Lance B. Eliot, MBA, PhD

<u>Chapter Title</u>

This title is available via Amazon and other book sellers

Companion Book By This Author

AI Self-Driving Cars Trendsetting

by Dr. Lance B. Eliot, MBA, PhD

This title is available via Amazon and other book sellers

<u>Companion Book By This Author</u>

AI Autonomous Cars
Forefront

by Dr. Lance B. Eliot, MBA, PhD

<u>Chapter Title</u>

This title is available via Amazon and other book sellers

Companion Book By This Author

AI Autonomous Cars Emergence

by Dr. Lance B. Eliot, MBA, PhD

This title is available via Amazon and other book sellers

<u>Companion Book By This Author</u>

AI Autonomous Cars Progress

by Dr. Lance B. Eliot, MBA, PhD

<u>Chapter Title</u>

This title is available via Amazon and other book sellers

Companion Book By This Author

AI Self-Driving Cars Prognosis

by Dr. Lance B. Eliot, MBA, PhD

This title is available via Amazon and other book sellers

ABOUT THE AUTHOR

Dr. Lance B. Eliot, MBA, PhD is the CEO of Techbruim, Inc. and Executive Director of the Cybernetic AI Self-Driving Car Institute, and has over twenty years of industry experience including serving as a corporate officer in a billion dollar firm and was a partner in a major executive services firm. He is also a serial entrepreneur having founded, ran, and sold several high-tech related businesses. He previously hosted the popular radio show *Technotrends* that was also available on American Airlines flights via their in-flight audio program. Author or co-author of a dozen books and over 400 articles, he has made appearances on CNN, and has been a frequent speaker at industry conferences.

A former professor at the University of Southern California (USC), he founded and led an innovative research lab on Artificial Intelligence in Business. Known as the "AI Insider" his writings on AI advances and trends has been widely read and cited. He also previously served on the faculty of the University of California Los Angeles (UCLA), and was a visiting professor at other major universities. He was elected to the International Board of the Society for Information Management (SIM), a prestigious association of over 3,000 high-tech executives worldwide.

He has performed extensive community service, including serving as Senior Science Adviser to the Vice Chair of the Congressional Committee on Science & Technology. He has served on the Board of the OC Science & Engineering Fair (OCSEF), where he is also has been a Grand Sweepstakes judge, and likewise served as a judge for the Intel International SEF (ISEF). He served as the Vice Chair of the Association for Computing Machinery (ACM) Chapter, a prestigious association of computer scientists. Dr. Eliot has been a shark tank judge for the USC Mark Stevens Center for Innovation on start-up pitch competitions, and served as a mentor for several incubators and accelerators in Silicon Valley and Silicon Beach. He served on several Boards and Committees at USC, including having served on the Marshall Alumni Association (MAA) Board in Southern California.

Dr. Eliot holds a PhD from USC, MBA, and Bachelor's in Computer Science, and earned the CDP, CCP, CSP, CDE, and CISA certifications. Born and raised in Southern California, and having traveled and lived internationally, he enjoys scuba diving, surfing, and sailing.

ADDENDUM

AI Self-Driving Cars Prognosis

Practical Advances in Artificial Intelligence (AI) and Machine Learning

By
Dr. Lance B. Eliot, MBA, PhD

For supplemental materials of this book, visit:

www.ai-selfdriving-cars.guru

For special orders of this book, contact:
LBE Press Publishing
Email: LBE.Press.Publishing@gmail.com